VIEnNA

— *in your pocket* —

MAIN CONTRIBUTOR: LOUIS JAMES

PHOTOGRAPH CREDITS
Photos supplied by The Travel Library:
Alan Copson 52, 55, 74, 86, 87, 112; Andrew Cowin title page, 5, 20, 27, 30, 31, 33, 34, 35, 38, 39, 42, 43, 44, 45, 47, 49, 50(t, b), 51, 53, 66, 67, 69, 70, 72, 75, 76(t, b), 82, 84, 89, 93, 95, 97, 103, 105, 111, 115, 119; Philip Enticknap front cover, 6, 18, 29, 37, 41, 48(b), 80, 123, 126; Christina Hamalainen 109; Jan Isachsen 8, 21, 48(t), 61, 63, 64, 99, 125; R Richardson 25, 57, 79; Alex Stephen 28, 32, 59, 60, 65.
Other Photos:
Austrian National Tourist Office back cover, 23, 36; Kunsthistorisches Museum, Vienna/Bridgeman Art Library, London 15, 56; Museo Real Academia de Bellas Artes, Madrid/Index/Bridgeman Art Library, London 11; Private Collection/Bridgeman Art Library, London 12; Österreichische Galerie, Vienna/Bridgeman Art Library, London 73.

Front cover: Fiaker in Michaelerplatz; back cover: Schloss Schönbrunn in winter; title page: detail of sculpture, the Hofburg.

MANUFACTURE FRANÇAISE DES PNEUMATIQUES MICHELIN
Place des Carmes-Déchaux – 63000 Clermont-Ferrand (France)
© Michelin et Cie. Propriétaires-Éditeurs 1998
Dépôt légal Avril 98 – ISBN 2-06-651901-4 – ISSN 1272-1689
No part of this publication may be reproduced in any form
without the prior permission of the publisher.
Printed in Spain 3-98

MICHELIN TYRE PLC
Tourism Department
The Edward Hyde Building
38 Clarendon Road
WATFORD Herts WD1 1SX - UK
☎ (01923) 415000

MICHELIN TRAVEL PUBLICATIONS
Editorial Department
One Parkway South
GREENVILLE, SC 29615
☎ 1-800 423-0485

CONTENTS

INTRODUCTION

Along the motorways at the approaches to
Vienna are posters with resonant slogans:
Wien ist anders (Vienna is different), or *Wien
bleibt Wien* (Vienna will always be Vienna).
This foretaste of the narcissistic image that
the Viennese like to project reminds us how
important are the images of collective
identity in Central Europe and especially in
this melting pot of a city. For Vienna also
radiates the past glory of a *Residenzstadt*: the
seat of Europe's longest enduring dynasty
and the capital of a far-reaching empire.

That a city living in the shadow of so much
history is lacking in the dynamism required
to confront the challenges of the modern
world was a constant refrain of the self-
critical Viennese themselves, especially in the
post-war years when the population of the
city slowly declined.

Nowadays, Vienna manages to be
remarkably up-to-date in many fields. For the
tourist, as for the local inhabitants, Vienna is
no longer a city seemingly dominated by the
middle-aged and pensioners. It has become
an increasingly lively environment, with a
burgeoning nightlife in the so-called
Bermuda Triangle of the Inner City, not to
mention its rediscovery of gastronomic
sophistication and the adoption of more
user-friendly shopping hours. Entry into the
European Union in January 1995 has also
brought Vienna more in line with European
consumer practices. These factors have
enhanced the traditional attractions that
have drawn so many visitors to Vienna over
the last hundred years: its unrivalled palette
of musical performances virtually every night
of the year; its lovely Gothic churches and

Baroque palaces; its *Heurigen* (taverns) in the wine villages nestling under the slopes of ancient vineyards; its Lipizzaners and Strauss waltzes; its Secessionist art (Gustav Klimt) or Otto Wagner's pioneering functional architecture; and finally its seductive Habsburg nostalgia.

At heart, however, Vienna remains in so many respects the village that Johannes Brahms said he preferred to live in, when giving his reasons for settling here. Even today, when the global village has so radically changed the perspective for most of us, the true-born Viennese feels the same way as Brahms.

The lovely Baroque Karlskirche was designed by local father and son architects, the Fischer von Erlachs.

BACKGROUND

GEOGRAPHY

Vienna (Wien) is situated at the north-eastern end of Austria, just east of the last spurs of the Alpine foothills, the area known as the **Wienerwald** (Vienna Woods). The **Danube**, once described by the preacher Abraham a Sancta Clara in the 17C as being like 'a roaring drunk', was tamed and

regulated in the late 19C. The **Danube Canal** (into which runs the River Wien itself) now flows between the Inner City (First District) and the Leopoldstadt (Second District). Further north is the Danube proper, divided into two arms, between them being a long, narrow island, a dedicated leisure area for the city's inhabitants. A branch of the 'Old Danube' is a favourite with bathers.

Tours and boat trips can be taken along the Danube Canal, into which flows the River Wien.

The historic **Innere Stadt** (Inner City) began as a Roman camp and extended gradually during the Middle Ages until it was enclosed by bastions in Renaissance times. Only in 1857 did Emperor Franz Joseph order their demolition, thus inaugurating the Ringstrasse boulevard, lined with Historicist public buildings such as the Opera, the Parliament, the Rathaus (City Hall), the Burgtheater and the Börse (Stock Exchange). Vienna (which is also one of the nine Austrian Federal States) now has 23 Districts, stretching from fashionable Hietzing with Schönbrunn in the south-west, to the outlying mostly working-class districts beyond the Danube, one of which contains the international UNO-City, with organisations such as UNIDO (International Industrial Development Organisation) and IAEO (International Atomic Energy Organisation).

One of the joys of Vienna is the architectural fabric's good state of preservation. This is part and parcel of the increasingly green policies pursued by the city fathers, which include the re-creation of traditional parks and the creation of new ones, tree-planting projects, conservation of Danubian fauna and flora as well as water-cleaning programmes, waste disposal and the use of environmentally-friendly fuel.

HISTORY

From Pre-History to the Babenbergs

The earliest inhabitants of the Vienna Basin (*Wiener Becken*) were **Celts**, who occupied the promontory on the Leopoldsberg to the west, before being removed to the plain by the **Romans**. The first settlements exploited the intersection of the Danube here, providing a North-South trade route, but the Romans also built 'Vindobona' into a military base. When they withdrew in AD 400 the area was repeatedly overrun in the era of the great migrations, until some stability was achieved by Charlemagne and his successors.

In 976 Emperor Otto II bestowed the Eastern March of the Empire on the Margraves of Babenberg, who were elevated to Dukes in 1156. For 270 years the **Babenbergs** ruled what had now acquired the name 'Ostarrichi', moving their residence to Vienna in 1156, where they established their court in the area still known as 'Am Hof'. Under Leopold V and Friedrich I of Babenberg, Vienna was a glittering ducal seat that attracted the great *Minnesänger* (singer-poets) of the day, such as Walther von der Vogelweide and Tannhäuser. It also grew rich from the institution of the staple right (compelling foreign merchants to offer their goods for sale in the city), and more dubiously from the huge ransom paid for the release of England's Richard Coeur-de-Lion, imprisoned on his way back from the Third Crusade.

The remains of a Roman encampment have been excavated in Michaelerplatz.

The Early Habsburgs

Following the death of the last Babenberg, the Bohemian claimant to Austria was defeated (1278) by Rudolf of Habsburg at Dürnkrut, north of Vienna on the Marchfeld, thus inaugurating 640 years of **Habsburg rule** that ended only in the aftermath of the First World War.

Distinguished early Habsburgs included **Albrecht II** (1330-1358), under whom the Albertine Choir of the cathedral was begun, and **Rudolf IV** 'the Founder', so-called because he founded the university and began the construction of the great South Tower (*Steffl*) of St Stephen's. Yet the early Habsburg period was also one of great natural disasters – in particular, fire and plague – which stimulated religious excess.

Under the able **Friedrich III** (1439-1493), who was the last Holy Roman Emperor to be crowned in Rome (1452), Vienna became prosperous after the currency was stabilised and the city raised to a bishopric. However, the 15C impact of heretical Hussite doctrines (originating with John Wycliffe and developed by the Bohemian Jan Hus) was to be succeeded by the almost total (but temporary) triumph of the **Reformation**, spear-headed by Protestant nobles. By the mid-16C, four-fifths of the population were Protestant, and even a Habsburg ruler (Maximilian II) was suspected of Protestant sympathies. The dynasty's commitment to Rome was demonstrated by **Ferdinand I**'s invitation to the Jesuits to settle in Vienna in 1551. This marked the beginning of the **Counter-Reformation** in Austria, which was expressed through the cultural propaganda of spectacles, theatre, sermonising and highly ornamented ecclesiastical architecture.

The Habsburgs

The Habsburgs became the most powerful dynasty in Europe through Maximilian I's 'marriage-bed diplomacy', ('Other nations make war, you, happy Austria, marry!', as a famous aphorism has it). In two and a half centuries, a family of relatively obscure German counts, who took their title from a Swiss estate (the Habichtsburg, or Hawk's Castle, on the Wülpersberg, later part of Switzerland) had become the rulers of 'an Empire on which the sun never set'. This was literally true, since at Karl V's accession the Empire included Spain and her South American possessions, as well as the Netherlands, Naples, Sicily and the hereditary Austrian lands. In 1521 he divided this inheritance with his brother, Ferdinand I, who received the Central European 'German' territories, and then inherited Bohemia and Hungary after the king of these countries was killed fighting the Turks in 1526.

Like his forebears since 1438, Ferdinand also became Holy Roman Emperor (1556). This increasingly honorary title was (with one short interlude) to be retained by the German branch of the family until Napoleon compelled Franz II to give it up in 1806 – by which time it had long referred, in Voltaire's phrase, to something that was 'neither Roman, nor Holy, nor an Empire'. The Spanish branch of the Habsburgs died out in 1700.

The Habsburgs were traditionally pious and maintained a successful alliance between throne and altar that did much to cement their power, although relations with the papacy were brought to breaking point by the ecclesiastical reforms ruthlessly imposed by the rationalist Emperor Joseph II (1780-1790). By the end of the 19C, the dynasty had come to be regarded as an anachronism, and in particular the nationalist and liberal spirit of the day undermined the principle of absolute monarchical rule adhered to in spirit (despite concessions) by the penultimate Emperor Franz Joseph, whose reign of 68 years ended in 1916. The First World War (initiated by Franz Joseph with a declaration of war against Serbia, in consequence of the assassination of the Crown Prince Franz Ferdinand) swept away not only the dynasty, but also its great experiment in governance, the last formulation of which was the Austro-Hungarian Empire (or Dual monarchy) set up in 1867. Intended to appease Hungarian aspirations to autonomy which were legitimised by ancient rights and privileges, this solution succeeded only in inflaming Slav nationalism, while failing to satisfy all the Magyar demands. Yet it brought a degree of stability and the rule of law to the Emperor's sprawling patchwork of dominions, benefits that have been more sympathetically valued with hindsight.

Emperor Maximilian I and family.

However, Vienna was by then facing another threat: in 1529 the Turkish Sultan's armies besieged the city for the first time. It was successfully defended by Count Salm, and in the years that followed a huge *tracé italien* (starwork fortification) was built round the old medieval town as a precautionary measure.

The Counter-Reformation

During the Counter-Reformation, from the mid-16C, Vienna experienced its second great influx of religious orders, adding to the substantial number who had been there since the Middle Ages. The great Gothic churches (Maria am Gestade, Stephansdom, the Augustinerkirche and the Church of the Teutonic Knights) were now supplemented by daringly executed Baroque ones, such as the Servite Church, Lukas von Hildebrandt's Peterskirche, and finally Fischer von Erlach's 18C masterpiece of the Karlskirche.

Despite the cost of lavish spectacles and his extensions to the Hofburg (once resulting in near-bankruptcy), **Leopold I** (1657-1705) survived the second and last Turkish siege of 1683, but only because Christendom came to the rescue with an army led by John Sobieski of Poland and the Duke of Lorraine, among whose officers was a dynamic warrior, **Prince Eugene of Savoy**. It was his armies that subsequently drove the Turks from the Empire and he was rewarded well enough to be able to engage Lukas von Hildebrandt to build his fabulous Belvedere Palace (1722), now the home of the Austrian Gallery and the Austrian Baroque Museum. For the Prince's winter use, Hildebrandt built a fine palace in the Inner City (1709 – it is now used by the Ministry of Finance).

With the Turkish threat finally banished, Vienna came into its own as an imperial '*Residenzstadt*'. The dynasty began to spend lavishly on building (Klosterneuburg, the Hofbibliothek, the Spanish Riding School, the Karlskirche under Karl VI, and Schönbrunn under his daughter, Maria Theresia).

Enlightened Absolutism, Reaction, Revolution

The age of enlightened absolutism, which began with **Maria Theresia**, saw an influx of able foreigners who planned and carried through educational, medical, legal and tax reforms. Vienna also became – and has remained – quintessentially a city of imperial (later state) employees, over 25 per cent of the inhabitants depending on the court for their livelihood in the 18C.

Joseph II, joint ruler with Maria Theresia until her death in 1780, is often regarded as the epitome of the enlightened absolute monarch – rational, authoritarian, anti-clerical (but not anti-religion, which was required to control the people) and anti-bigotry. His 1781 Edict of Tolerance promulgated the free practice of different religious faiths and lifted the most

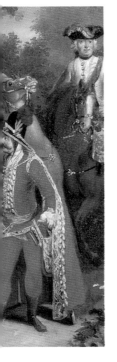

Joseph II (sole ruler 1780-1790) learning to ride at the age of six.

13

oppressive restrictions placed on the Jews. A reflection of the contemporary doctrines of the **Enlightenment** may also be seen in Mozart's opera *The Magic Flute* (1791), which was to become the favourite opera of the Viennese. Yet the roots struck by the Enlightenment were relatively shallow, partly due to the impatience of Emperor Joseph, of whom Frederick the Great remarked, 'He always took the second step before the first.' On his deathbed, the Emperor was obliged to repeal the vast majority of his often sensible but insensitively executed reforms.

After the brief rule of **Leopold II**, political reaction set in with the reign of **Franz II** (1792-1835), whose principal adviser was Prince Metternich. Following the Napoleonic wars (in which Franz was humiliated and even had to marry off his daughter to the ambitious young Napoleon) an age of repression and censorship was ushered in with the **Congress of Vienna** (1814).

Metternich succeeded for some 30 years in re-establishing and securing the old order; the Emperor's subjects withdrew into the politically harmless private pleasures of the **Biedermeier age**, a term referring to the middle-class solidity and somewhat idealised family life as reflected in contemporary arts and literature. Underneath the surface, however, the deprivation of bourgeois liberties and the hardship of an increasingly substantial urban working class were beginning to build up steam.

In 1848, stimulated by bad harvests and unemployment, revolution broke out all over the Empire. The simple-minded **Ferdinand I** of Austria (the new title adopted by the Habsburgs after the demise of the Holy Roman Empire) was forced to abdicate in favour of his nephew, the eighteen-year-old **Franz Joseph**. After indiscriminate reprisals against the revolutionaries, undertaken as soon as he felt strong enough to break the promises given to his peoples by Ferdinand, Franz Joseph set about ruling his Empire by decree.

As time went on, and dynastic power gradually weakened in the face of rising nationalism and the liberal demands of an emergent upper-middle class, he settled for a concessionary policy of muddling through (*fortwursteln*) which aimed to keep the nations of the Empire in what his Prime Minister (Count Taaffe) called 'a balanced condition of well-modulated discontent'.

Franz Joseph I, who became Emperor at the age of eighteen, ordered the destruction of Vienna's bastions in 1857, thus initiating the construction of the famous Ringstrasse.

The Ringstrassen Era

Franz Joseph's single most important act for Vienna was his decision in 1857 to demolish the fortifications of the old town and build a Haussmann-style boulevard on the cleared ground, which was to be flanked by the great representative buildings of the new financial class. In the **Ringstrassen era** that followed (also known as the *Gründerzeit* or Founder's Period), fortunes were made by developers

and speculators, and modernising Liberals
came to power in the City Hall.

The great financial crash of 1873 (also the
year that a World Exhibition was held in
Vienna) was a setback, but only a temporary
one. The waltzes of Johann Strauss and
frivolous operettas have come to symbolise
an age deluged in champagne and bad debts
co-existing with urban poverty.

The Two Republics

The First World War (initiated by Franz
Joseph with a declaration of war against
Serbia, in consequence of the assassination
of the Crown Prince Franz Ferdinand) swept
away not only the dynasty, but also its great
experiment in governance, the last
formulation of which was the Austro-
Hungarian Empire (or Dual monarchy) set
up in 1867. The institution of universal male
suffrage in 1907 gave impetus to the
increasing power of the Social Democrats,
led by the charismatic doctor, **Viktor Adler**.
When the Monarchy collapsed in the
aftermath of the First World War, the new
Republic of Austria was initially strongly
Socialist. Although national government
passed into the hands of the Christian
Socialists (i.e. Conservatives) and then to
clerico-Fascists, Vienna stayed red and has
returned a Socialist mayor at every free
election since 1919. In the 1920s '*Rotes Wien*'
embarked on a radical and ambitious
programme to provide housing and welfare,
using a steeply progressive local tax to raise
money. In the **Civil War** of 1934 the most
famous of the new blocks of social housing,
the Karl-Marx-Hof, was bombarded into
submission by Chancellor Dollfuss's troops.

In March 1938 Hitler marched into

Austria, declaring Vienna 'a pearl' that he wished to restore to its rightful place in the German Reich. Austrians soon discovered what this actually meant: they were to be used as cannon-fodder, and their country reduced to an insignificant *Gau* of the Third Reich. Of Vienna's 80 000 Jews, those who could not buy their freedom were shipped off to extermination camps.

After the end of the Second World War, the allies remained in occupation until the State Treaty of 1955 (signed in the Belvedere), during which period the Russians took the opportunity to remove the entire industrial infrastructure in their sector. Vienna had not suffered as badly as some German cities in the war but 20 per cent of its housing stock had been destroyed.

The **post-war reconstruction** began slowly, gathering momentum in the 1960s, and Austria gradually emerged as one of the most prosperous countries in Europe. The population declined until 1990 but has since begun to rise again. Under **Chancellor Bruno Kreisky** (1970-1983), Vienna became the third UNO centre, after New York and Geneva, and other international organisations (such as OPEC and the Organisation for Co-operation and Security in Europe) have found Austria's neutrality and her geographical position between East and West convenient. Meanwhile, there has also been an influx of mostly Slav guest workers (*Gastarbeiter*), employed in construction and service industries. Vienna is again a lively cosmopolitan city, where several cultures mingle and are gradually moulded into something that has become distinctively and incomparably 'Viennese'.

PEOPLE AND CULTURE

The Viennese are eclectic in racial origin,
but they have produced a remarkably
homogeneous culture. This achievement – a
self-confirmation born out of individual
struggle and rejection – is one reason why
Vienna is such a narcissistic city, selling itself
with slogans and marketing campaigns that
stress the city's unique charm and the so-
called 'golden Viennese heart'.

However, the Viennese are by no means
always charming and the image they present
to the outsider hides a mass of
contradictions. They have always been (and
still are) extremely religious; yet preachers
and foreigners alike have
castigated them for their
loose morals, and for
their *Schlamperei* or
sloppiness (Mahler told
enraged members of the
opera orchestra that what
they claimed was sacred
Viennese tradition was
merely an excuse for
Schlamperei). The
difference between
image and reality in such
matters (between *Schein*
and *Sein*, as the locals
say) is what makes the
city both frustrating and
creative, where the
malcontent is an artist
and as likely as not the
artist is a professional
malcontent.

At heart the Viennese
are profoundly

conservative, attached to rituals such as visits to the *Heurigen* (wine taverns) where fizzy young wine is sold and maudlin songs are sung. Quite often moody and *grantig* (grumpy), they are capable of sudden displays of affection and mordant humour. Respectful of authority, in private the Viennese can be bitterly contemptuous of all the megalomaniac follies committed by the bosses and politicians. They want to be loved, but intrigue and backbiting are second nature to them. In short, it is very difficult for a Viennese to live in his native city; but it is even more difficult for him to live without it.

Music is everywhere in Vienna; here street musicians perform in the Kohlmarkt.

The Arts

Since Austria once again became free after the Second World War, Vienna has set about rebuilding its cultural heritage. The Wiener Philharmoniker remains one of the best-loved orchestras in the world, and the famous New Year's Day concert broadcast from the Musikverein reminds huge audiences spread over many lands that Vienna is, in many respects, still the music capital of the world.

There are several arts festivals during the year (the best-known is the Wiener Festwochen, mid-May to mid-June) and all the theatres in the city are handsomely subsidised by the state or the municipality. Add to this a broad palette of major art exhibitions, jazz and film festivals, centenary composer festivals, and much more, and Karl Kraus's sardonic observation seems as true today as it was when he made it: 'The streets of Vienna are covered with culture as the streets of other cities are covered with asphalt.'

Baroque Vienna

Initially it was Italian architects, artists, librettists and composers who were the carriers of the Baroque idea to Vienna. Baroque art was emotional and dramatic, making liberal use of chiaroscuro or trompe l'oeil effects. The most vivid examples of religious Baroque combine narrative and doctrinal power, as in Lorenzo Mattielli's astonishing stucco in the Peterskirche, showing St John Nepomuk being thrown into the Moldau, or the Plague Column on the Graben, raised to mark deliverance from the 1679 epidemic.

Secular Baroque also began with great palaces built by Italians such as Tencala and Martinelli, but the second phase brought an indigenous style to the city, with the works of Fischer von Erlach (father and son), Lukas von Hildebrandt, and artists such as Franz Anton Maulbertsch and sculptors like Georg Raphael Donner (creator of the Providentia Fountain on the Neuer Markt). The main function of secular Baroque was to glorify the great princes and aristocrats who commissioned it, and who were celebrated in the complicated imagery of the decoration which compared them to the heroes of antiquity. Last, but not least, the Emperors themselves (notably Leopold I) laid on huge spectacles in the Hofburg featuring equine ballets, ships floating on artificial lakes and fireworks (80 000 were used at the celebration of Leopold's marriage to the Spanish Infanta). Even Maria Theresia, who tried to bring some order into the Habsburg's financial affairs, nevertheless insisted that there 'must be *spectacles* – a *Residenz* requires that'.

Left: Peterskirche. Right: Providentia Fountain.

Architecture

Crucial to the development of architecture
in Vienna has been the influence of
religious orders, both under the Babenbergs
and the Habsburgs. It is one of the reasons
that Vienna flourished as an artistic centre:
there were always churches to be built or
altered, religious paintings to be
commissioned and requiems, masses and
motets to be composed.

Vienna acquired a reputation for enjoying
good living in the Middle Ages. The **Gothic**
blossomed in Vienna as elsewhere in
Europe, as the religious orders rebuilt the
low, solid Romanesque churches in the new
style, with lofty vaulted ceilings, slender
pillars, tall windows with pointed arches and
stained-glass windows, and light interiors
which appeared to reach into the heavens.

The **Renaissance** was not to have the
impact in Vienna that it enjoyed elsewhere,
not least because the city was seemingly
constantly under threat, not only from the
Turks but also from plague and fire.
Nevertheless, it has some fine examples,
notably the Schweizertor and the Stallburg
in the Hofburg.

When the threat of Turkish invasion
receded in 1683, the city entered its **Golden
Age of Baroque**. Splendid palaces were built,
together with mansions, public buildings
and churches, turning Vienna into a
magnificent imperial city (*see* p20).

When Vienna became a *Residenzstadt* there
were further opportunities for patronage,
since the aristocracy clustered round the
court (hence the name 'Herrengasse', the
'Street of the Lords', which runs to the
north-west of the Hofburg). Building space
limited secular architectural commissions,

until the fading of the Turkish menace emboldened the nobility to compete with the emperors and build magnificent summer palaces beyond the city walls.

A reflection of the Enlightenment in the late 18C was the individual style of the **Biedermeier age**, which lasted from 1814-1848. Perhaps the greatest mark on the city was left in the mid-19C, with Franz Joseph's clearance of the old town's fortifications. He replaced them with the grand **Ringstrasse**, flanked by impressive Historicist buildings. Vienna's architectural development was completed with the **Secessionist** buildings of Wagner and Olbrich.

Music

At least from the time of the Babenberg Dukes in the 12C, when the *Minnesänger* sang of courtly love, Vienna has been a centre of great music. This long tradition, which always included a rich layer of popular song, dance and folk music running parallel to courtly music, was given impetus both by the Habsburg court and by the church: in Vienna, the market for masses has usually been just as strong as that for operas. More than one emperor was himself a composer, and as early as 1493 Maximilian I founded the famous **Vienna Boys Choir** (*Wiener Sängerknaben*) which, to this day, performs a sung mass on Sundays in the Burgkapelle of the Hofburg.

The first great modern flowering of Viennese music was in the Baroque period, when Pietro Metastasio was the court poet

Performances of the world famous Vienna Boys Choir, which dates back to 1493, are always very popular.

and the much maligned **Antonio Salieri**
(1750-1823) was the court composer. The
latter composed some 40 operas and his
distinguished pupils included Beethoven,
Schubert and Liszt, although he is best
remembered for the false story (resurrected
in the play *Amadeus*) that he poisoned his
rival, Mozart.

The great change from the highly artificial
Italian style in opera (long recitatives, over-
ornamented arias) came with **Christoph
Willibald Gluck** (1714-1787), whose major
works (the most famous is *Orfeo ed Euridice*)
have remained in the repertoire. In 1781,
Wolfgang Amadeus Mozart settled in Vienna
and brought the Vienna classic form
developed by his mentor and admirer,
Joseph Haydn (1732-1809), to its highest
degree of originality and refinement.
Although he had difficulties in Vienna, the
public took *The Magic Flute* to its heart, the
opera's adroit mixture of profundity and
near farce appealing greatly to the Viennese
temperament. **Ludwig van Beethoven** lived
and worked in Vienna from 1792 until his
death in 1827, receiving generous
commissions from the local nobility.

The native **Franz Schubert** (1797-1828),
however, gained little recognition in his own
lifetime. Like Haydn before him, he had
been a member of the Vienna Boys Choir
and his music is steeped in local tradition
and ambience. In particular, he wrote
chamber music and *Lieder* of unparalleled
beauty, and pieces such as *The Trout* or the
song-cycle *Die Winterreise* for which posterity
has honoured him, but which were known to
only a small circle of his contemporaries.

The late 19C saw two great musical rivals
in the city: the profoundly pious and highly

original **Anton Bruckner**, and the most refined exponent of romantic classicism, **Johannes Brahms**, a German from Hamburg. Vicious backbiting and factionalism was evident at this time, there being a 'Wagnerian' group that chose Bruckner as its hero and a traditionalist group which favoured Brahms.

Antagonism and malice reached a sort of apotheosis in the treatment of **Gustav Mahler** (1860-1911), who was finally driven from his post as the musical director of the opera by a mixture of intrigue, press smears and anti-Semitism. **Arnold Schönberg** (1874-1951) and the protagonists of his atonality and twelve-note system fared little better. Schönberg's pupils included **Alban Berg** and **Anton von Webern**.

The counter-image of Vienna as a carefree city of 'wine, women and song' has its origin in the waltzes of **Joseph Lanner** and **Johann Strauss** (father and son), together with the music of numerous turn-of-the-century operetta composers – (**Franz Lehár** is perhaps the best known). The spirit of operetta is also present in the German-born **Richard Strauss**'s romantic opera *Der Rosenkavalier* (1911), a tale of amorousness, lust and idealised love set in 18C Vienna, lushly orchestrated and full of ironically depicted Viennese sentimentality.

There are reminders of Mozart throughout the city; this statue, by Viktor Tilgner, is in the Burggarten.

MUST SEE

The Hofburg★★★
The Hofburg is almost a small town in itself, with 18 wings, 54 stairways and around 2 600 rooms. Sights include the **Kaiserappartements★** (Imperial Apartments), the **Weltliche und geistliche Schatzkammer★★★** (Sacred and Secular Treasuries), the Chapel, the **Spanische Reitschule★★** (Spanish Riding School) and the beautiful **Österreichische National-bibliothek★** (Court Library).

Schloss Schönbrunn★★★
(Schönbrunn Palace)
Although on the western out-skirts of the city, most visitors will want to see the magnificent imperial summer palace of the Habsburgs. Tours include some of the 1 441 lavish rooms, such as the **Great Gallery★★★**. The landscaped **Park★★** contains the **Palmenhaus★** (Palm House) and **Tiergarten★** (Zoo), with the colonnaded pavilion of the **Gloriette★★** set on a mound overlooking the grounds and palace, with superb views.

Stephansdom★★★
(St Stephen's Cathedral)
and **Graben★**
The heart and soul of the city since medieval times, **Stephansdom★★★** is one of the finest Gothic buildings in Central Europe. You can climb the soaring **South Tower★★★** and visit the catacombs, but the major sights in the cathedral itself are the **pulpit★★** by Franz Anton Pilgram and the late Gothic **tomb of Friedrich III★★**. In the 19C, courtesans known as *Grabennymphen* used to importune cavaliers on the **Graben★**, but now it is the most fashionable street in Vienna. At the centre is the magnificent **Pestsäule★★** (Plague Column), partly designed by Fischer von Erlach, and just to the east, the **Peterskirche★** by Lukas von Hildebrandt, with superb stucco work by Lorenzo Mattielli.

Schloss Belvedere★★
Built for the Habsburgs' greatest general, Prince Eugene of Savoy, the Belvedere Palace is the finest and most ambitious example of secular Baroque architecture in the region. It includes the **Lower Belvedere★**, with the **Österreichisches Barockmuseum★★** (Baroque Museum) and the **Museum Mittelalterlicher Österreichischer Kunst★** (Museum of Medieval Art) in the Orangery, a beautiful park with Alpine and Botanical Gardens attached, and the

imposing **Upper Belvedere★★**, housing the **Österreichische Galerie★★** (Austrian Art Gallery).

Karlskirche★★ and Karlsplatz★★

The most notable work of the local Baroque architects Johann Bernhard Fischer von Erlach and his son, Joseph Emanuel, the church dedicated to St Carlo Borromeo dominates the **Karlsplatz★★**. Lit up on a snowy winter's evening it is an unforgettable sight, with its great dome rising beyond the massive Trajanesque columns at the front.

Secession★★

Joseph Maria Olbrich's idiosyncratic exhibition hall was created for the artists of the Viennese Secession in 1897. It contains Gustav Klimt's remarkable **Beethoven Frieze★★★** and is used for exhibitions of contemporary art. Since its restoration it is once again resplendent, a Viennese landmark that stands out against the bombastic Ringstrassen architecture in its neighbourhood.

An impressive dome surmounts the Michaelertrakt in the Hofburg.

Kunsthistorisches Museum★★★
(Museum of Art History)
One of the greatest collections in Europe, the museum includes not only a superb gallery of pictures acquired by the Habsburgs, but also the unique collections of applied art, coins and antiquities.

Freyung★
This delightful area is flanked by places of great interest for the visitor: the **Schottenstift★** (Monastery of the Scots), with its cloister gallery and the medieval **Schottenaltar★★** (altarpiece), the magnificent Baroque palaces of the Harrach and Kinsky families, and the Freyung arcade designed by Heinrich Ferstel, attached to which is the legendary Café Central. Seven centuries of history are here harmoniously merged in the characteristic Viennese manner.

Grinzing★
One could choose from a large number of Heurigen villages, with their wine taverns, but **Grinzing★** remains the most charming. At night, its Biedermeier houses and narrow streets are bathed in soft yellow lamplight and the sounds of *Schrammelmusik* waft from the open windows of the taverns. The village's nostalgic charm and the dirndled waitresses radiating the 'golden Viennese heart' make Grinzing hard to resist.

Prater★
This huge area, once an imperial hunting ground, is now home to the vast funfair known as the **Wurstelprater**, dominated by the great **Riesenrad★★** (Ferris Wheel). Visitors of all ages will find something to amuse here, from roundabouts and dodgems to entertainers such as sword-swallowers and magicians.

The grand stairway of the Kunsthistorisches Museum.

THE HOFBURG★★★

The impressive collection of buildings
known as the Hofburg (JR), home to the
Habsburgs from the 13C, represents a blend
of architectural styles from the Gothic,
through Renaissance to late-19C
Historicism, as each generation added to the
complex. The earliest fortress on the site was
constructed by Przemysl Otakar II of
Bohemia, in 1275, in anticipation of attack
by his Habsburg rival for Austria. It stood on
the ground on which the Schweizerhof now
stands.

It is a good idea to orient yourself first by
standing '**In der Burg**' before exploring the
complex of buildings. This is the central
courtyard, reached from the Michaelerplatz
to the north-east or the Heldenplatz to the

*A statue of Kaiser
Franz I stands in
the central
courtyard of the
Hofburg, known as
'In der Burg'.*

The grandiose entrance to the Hofburg is even more impressive when illuminated at night.

south-west. Facing north-west, the oldest part is behind you, while to the left is the **Leopoldinischer Trakt**, the wing built under Leopold I. The Renaissance **Amalienburg** (1575) is in front and the **Reichskanzleitrakt** (1723-1730 – built for the officials of the Holy Roman Empire) is to the right. Behind is the **Schweizerhof**, with the Sacred and Secular Treasuries at the south-east end and

Neo-Baroque sculptures symbolising victories at sea and on land adorn the walls of the Hofburg.

the **Burgkapelle** at the south-west. If you continue through the Schweizerhof and go through a passage at the far side, you emerge onto **Josefsplatz**, on the right-hand side of which is the **Österreichische Nationalbibliothek** (National Library). The continuation of the wing through which you have emerged contains the **Redoute** (once a ballroom, now mostly used for conferences and recently restored after a serious fire in 1992), and beyond it the **Winterreitschule** (Winter Riding School), where the famous Lipizzaners perform their horse ballets. Across the road from the school is the arcaded Renaissance **Stallburg** (Imperial Stables), where the Lipizzaners live in the comfort befitting employees of the Austrian state.

The entrance to the **Kaiserappartements★**

(Imperial Apartments) and the **Imperial Tableware and Silver Collection★** (*open daily 9am-5pm*) is via the Kaisertor In der Burg. The tableware collection contains Augarten porcelain and Lobmeyr glass, and a 33m (108ft) long **centrepiece** used for state receptions. The tour of the Imperial Apartments used by Franz Joseph and Elisabeth goes through the audience chamber, Franz Joseph's bedroom (he rose at 4.20am every day), the cabinet room, Empress Elisabeth's dressing room with her gymnastic equipment, to the rooms occupied by Tsar Alexander I during the Congress of Vienna (1814-1815) and lastly, the splendid **Banqueting Hall**.

Leaving the apartments on the Ballhausplatz, walk round to the Michaelerplatz to reach your starting point. Once again starting from In der Burg, go through the **Schweizertor** (Swiss Gate),

Fit for a king – the State Banqueting Room as it would have appeared in Franz Joseph's time.

surmounted by the coat of arms of
Ferdinand I listing his titles (1552); to the
rear of the Schweizertor on the right is the
Renaissance **Burgkapelle** (Hofburg Chapel),
built in 1449 under Friedrich III.
(*Tickets for Sunday's mass sung by the Vienna
Boys Choir are available on the preceding Friday
from 5-6pm. Otherwise the chapel is usually open
from 1.30-3.30pm, except in July and August.*)

Below the chapel is the entrance to the
Weltliche und geistliche Schatzkammer★★★
(Secular and Sacred Treasuries). They
contain some magnificent treasures relating
to the Holy Roman Empire, including a
Holy Lance from the 8C, a stunning 10C
Imperial Crown★★★, an agate bowl claimed
to be the Holy Grail, and something long
thought to be the horn of a unicorn

*The equestrian
statue of Joseph II
stands majestically
in Josefsplatz, with
the Prunksaal of the
Österreichische
Nationalbibliothek
behind.*

(actually a narwhal tusk). The Sacred Treasury's exhibits include fine monstrances and reliquary holders, as well as the penitential scourges used by the pious Empress Anna (1585-1618). (*Open Wed-Mon 10am-6pm, Thur 10am-9pm.*)

Continuing through the passageway, you emerge into the **Josefsplatz★** (with an equestrian statue in the centre presenting Joseph II as a Roman Emperor, and enter to your right the **Österreichische Nationalbibliothek★** (National Library). The library was built by Johann Fischer von Erlach and his son, Joseph Emanuel, for Karl VI and was completed in 1735. Note the Baroque sculpture of Minerva above the façade, and the Atlas figures on the roof added in 1880. In the library's **Prunksaal★★** (Ceremonial Hall) are marble statues of Karl VI and other Habsburgs by Peter and Paul Strudel, while the cupola frieze by Daniel Gran represents *The Apotheosis of Karl VI.*

The restored figures on the roof of the Österreichische Nationalbibliothek.

Entrance to the **Winterreitschule** (Winter Riding School) on the north side of the square is now gained from a gangway In der Burg, beside the Schweizertor, where times of performances are posted. The famous Lipizzaners of the **Spanische Reitschule**★★ (Spanish Riding School) perform their stylised ballet-like dressage to music, the movements having their origin in the battle tactics of cavalry horses. The name of the Lipizzaners comes from the stud at Lipizza, now in Slovenia, where the tough karst horses once used in the chariot races in

Sculpture of two caryatids forming the portal of a Josefsplatz palace.

A supreme display of horsemanship and equestrian skills at the Spanish Riding School.

Rome were cross-bred with Spanish thoroughbreds (hence 'Spanish' Riding School) from the late 16C.
(*Tickets for 'morning training' and performances are available from ticket agencies, but for the performances it is advisable to book well in advance from the Spanische Reitschule A-1010 Josefsplatz 1, Wien.*)

Around the Hofburg

To the south-west of the old Burg is the huge curving façade of the **Neue Burg** (JR), completed only in 1913. It was from the balcony here that Hitler harangued jubilant crowds in 1938. It houses the National Library, the **Museum für Völkerkunde★** (Ethnology Museum), the **Sammlung alter Musikinstrumente★★** (Collections of Old

A traditional fiaker sets off from the Neue Burg on a tour of the sights of Vienna.

Musical Instruments) and the **Waffensammlung**★ (Weapons Collection), as well as the **Ephesos Museum**★★. On the **Heldenplatz**★, which it overlooks, are heroic neo-Baroque equestrian statues of Prince Eugene of Savoy and Archduke Carl, respectively successful in battle against the Turks and the Napoleonic forces.

To the north of the Hofburg is the **Michaelerplatz**★ with the fine **Michaelerkirche** (St Michael's Church), notable for the fabulous stucco over the main altar which shows St Michael casting out rebellious angels from heaven (Karl Georg Merville, 1782). In the passage to the south of the church is a limestone relief of *Christ on the Mount of Olives* (1494). The other important feature of the

Michaelerplatz is the **Loos-Haus**, the so-called 'house without eyebrows', built by Adolf Loos in 1912. It caused a stir as it lacked the traditional lintels and sills, or any ornaments. (*It is now a bank, but access is allowed from 8am-5pm, longer when exhibitions are in progress on the first floor.*) Just beyond the Loos-Haus, on the Kohlmarkt, is the famous **Demel** coffee-house and confectioner.

To the south-east of the Hofburg, adjoining the Josefsplatz, is the former parish church for the Burg, the austerely Gothic **Augustinerkirche**. The rather sparse interior (after 're-Gothicisation' by Ferdinand von Hohenberg at the turn of the 19C) has a striking **tomb★** (1805) for Maria Theresia's favourite daughter, Marie

As dusk falls, Heldenplatz takes on a new beauty.

The astonishing Baroque stucco behind the altar in Michaelerkirche shows the angels being cast from heaven.

Christine, designed by **Antonio Canova**. The
Loreto Chapel contains the hearts of several
Habsburg rulers in silver urns.

At the eastern end of the church is the
Albertinaplatz (JR) named after Marie
Christine's husband, who built up the great
collection of prints and drawings in the
Albertina★★ itself (*currently closed for
restoration*). In the middle of the square is
Alfred Hrdlicka's striking **Monument against
War and Fascism**, erected in 1988 on the
50th anniversary of Hitler's invasion of
Austria. To the north-east is the lovely
Lobkowitz Palais, bought in 1753 by Prince
Wenzel Lobkowitz, a patron of Beethoven,
and boasting a dignified Baroque façade by
Fischer von Erlach. It houses part of the
Österreichisches Theatermuseum (Austrian
Theatre Museum) and is worth a visit for the
palace's fine interior, quite apart from the
exhibits, which include Alfred Roller's
Secessionist stage sets dating from Gustav
Mahler's directorship of the opera.

STEPHANSDOM★★★
(ST STEPHEN'S CATHEDRAL)

This is the focal point of Viennese life and
history, which explains why all the provinces
of Austria gave money to repair it after the
war. The earliest church on the site of the
Stephansdom (KR) was Romanesque
(1147), and was just outside the city
boundaries at that time. The two
Romanesque towers at the west end date to
reconstruction in 1263, following a fire.

The most notable Gothic architectural
features are the **Albertine Choir** with its
beautiful vaulting (completed 1340), and
the great **South Tower★★★** (known as the

*St Stephen's
Cathedral has been
the heart of Vienna
since the Middle
Ages, and remains a
landmark today
with its distinctive
tiled roof and the
great South Tower.*

'Steffl'), which took 74 years to build (1359-1433) from the time the first sod was turned by Rudolf the Founder (1339-65). Rudolf and his consort lie in a tomb inside the cathedral on the north wall of the choir. The 137m (450ft) spire can be climbed by stairs as far as **Starhemberg's seat**, named after the city commander in 1683, who watched the manoeuvres of the besieging Turks from here, and where the visitor can still enjoy the panorama. The **North** or **Adler Tower**, never completed, was capped with a Renaissance lantern in 1566. It houses the famous huge **Pummerin Bell**, which can be reached by lift.

Anton Pilgram's famous pulpit in St Stephen's.

Tombs and Gothic carvings adorn the exterior of the cathedral (though they are badly in need of cleaning) and the striking tiled roof shows a pattern of yellow and black chevrons. Against the north-east wall, on the site where the Dominican Giovanni Capistrano delivered fire-and-brimstone sermons against the Turks in the mid-15C, is a later pulpit. The preacher himself took part in the victorious Battle of Belgrade (1456) and died of exhaustion shortly after.

Not to be missed in the interior of St Stephen's is the late-Gothic **pulpit★★** (circa 1500) attributed to Anton Pilgram, who has portrayed himself under the pulpit steps, as if leaning out of a window. On the side panels are portraits of Saints Ambrose, Jerome, Augustine and Gregory (fathers of the church), who are interestingly depicted as the four humours (phlegm, blood, choler and black bile) that determined the human

temperament in the philosophy of the
Middle Ages. You can see another Pilgram
self-portrait in the figure under the stone
ribs of the organ loft, to the north.

Passing the entrance to the **catacombs**
(where the embalmed entrails of the
Habsburg rulers were deposited) you come
to the end of the north aisle. In
front is the elaborate **Wiener
Neustädter Altar★** (1447), the
decoration depicting various saints
and scenes from the lives of Christ
and the Virgin Mary. The Baroque
painting of the high altar shows
the *Stoning of St Stephen* (Tobias
and Johann Pock, 1640), and
marble figures of Saints Leopold
(the Babenburg founder of local
monasteries), Florian (the
protector against fire), and Rochus
and Sebastian (both protectors
against plague), all made by
Tobias's brother, Johann Jakob.

In the southern apse is the
Tomb of Emperor Friedrich III★★,
superb late-Gothic work mostly by Niclas
Gerhaert van Leyden. Steps at the back lead
onto the balustrade surrounding it, so that
the cathedral canons could process round
the tomb singing and praying.
(*A complete guided tour is available for those
interested in the many other Gothic, Renaissance
and Baroque details of the cathedral, and a
separate tour explores the catacombs.*)

The nearby **Dom- und Diözesanmuseum★**
in **Stephansplatz★★** has an interesting
collection of ecclesiastical art treasures and
possesses a celebrated **Portrait of Rudolf the
Founder★★**, painted in the year of his death
(1365), and representing the earliest

*The past blends
with the present in
Vienna, as a
costumed figure
strolls across
Stephensplatz, with
the ultra modern
Haas-Haus behind.*

surviving royal portrait in Central Europe.

Diagonally across Stephansplatz is the controversial **Haas-Haus**, designed by Hans Hollein (1990). The shining curved glass and blue marble façade is uncompromisingly modern, but is an aesthetic success in this architecturally sensitive setting, and leads the visitor from the square into the Graben.

THE GRABEN★

The original Roman *urbs quadrata* of Vindobona was protected on every side by natural defences, such as streams or the drop to the Danube shore, except to the south-west. The three lines of ditches that were a necessary defence here gave the

The elegant Graben leads down to the Plague Column, built to give thanks for the city's deliverance from the 1679 epidemic.

Graben (JR) its name. Today, it is the most elegant street of the Inner City, with bookshops, an Italian-style coffee-house and the fashionable **Lehmann Konditorei**.

Its focal point is the **Pestsäule**★★ (Plague Column), also known as the Holy Trinity Column, which stands at the mid-point. It was raised by Leopold I in thanksgiving for deliverance from the 1679 epidemic. On its lower south section is a vivid sculpture of Leopold, kneeling in prayer. The symbolism of the monument combines references to the Holy Trinity, with symbols of the three pillars of Habsburg power – Bohemia, Hungary and Austria.

To the north is the 18C **Peterskirche**★ (St Peter's Church), built to an original plan by Lukas von Hildebrandt, an ingeniously

The lovely Baroque Peterskirche is adroitly fitted into a tiny site, yet the dome is 56m in diameter.

compact solution to fit the confined site.
The most notable work in the **interior**★ is
Lorenzo Mattielli's gilded stucco of **St John
of Nepomuk being thrown into the Moldau**,
on the orders of Wenceslas II (he had
refused to reveal to the King the secrets of
the Queen's confession; *see* p20).

A little to the south-east of Stephansdom,
at Singerstrasse 7, is another historic church,
the **Deutschordenskirche** (Church of the
Teutonic Knights). The inside of the Gothic
church is lined with red marble tombstones
of the Grand Masters of the Order. The
Schatzkammer★ (Treasury) is also worth a
visit, and is reached through a courtyard at
the rear (*limited opening times – check the notice
on the door or* ☎ *512 10 65*). It contains a rich
collection of the **knights' treasures**★,
including silver objects, medals, coins and
paintings.

THE RINGSTRASSE★★

Until the 19C, the old city of Vienna was
girdled by Renaissance fortifications. In
1857 Emperor Franz Joseph was persuaded
by his minister, Alexander Freiherr von
Bach, to have these razed and to build a
boulevard, **Ringstrasse** (hereafter 'the
Ring'), on the Parisian model. This passed
through an area just outside the old
bastions, where formerly there had been
military exercise and parade grounds.

The new buildings of the Ringstrasse
represented the political and cultural
aspirations of emergent Liberalism. They
were built in the symbolic styles of
Historicism, as appropriate to their
functions: neo-Classical for the Parliament,
alluding to the ancient cradle of democracy;

neo-Gothic for the City Hall, alluding to the free burgher cities of the Middle Ages; neo-Renaissance for the University, and so on. All these monumental edifices were built between 1860 and 1890.

From Schwedenplatz it is possible to take a tram round the Ring in either direction (*No 1 clockwise, No 2 anti-clockwise*), but it is more fun to walk the circle, as Sigmund Freud regularly did (about 4.5km/2.8 miles). The first sight in a clockwise direction from Schwedenplatz is the former **Regierungsgebäude** (War Ministry) (LR), with the equestrian statue of Field Marshal Radetzky in front of it. He was the greatest Austrian general of the 19C, winning a number of important victories against rebellious Italians in 1848, and thereafter remaining as Governor of the Italian

A monument to Georg Coch, founder of the Austrian Post Office Savings Bank, stands in front of Otto Wagner's famous Secession Postsparkasse (1912).

provinces into his dotage. Opposite the statue, set back on Georg-Coch-Platz, is Otto Wagner's **Postsparkasse★** (Post Office Savings Bank, 1912), one of the most famous examples of his functional Secession style (*see* p72).

The next buildings on the south side of the Ring are the High School for Applied Art and the **Museum für Angewandte Kunst★★** (Museum of Applied Art), commonly known as MAK. It contains a large collection of Austrian applied art, of which the Biedermeier (1814–1848) and **Wiener Werkstätte★★** items are among the most interesting. In addition,

Detail of the Strauss Monument in the Stadtpark.

The Staatsoper, one of the world's leading opera houses.

there are Medieval European, Asian and Oriental collections. Representative examples from each section of the museum are exhibited in special individual rooms, each display having been designed by a different contemporary artist.

As you continue west, you reach the delightful **Stadtpark** (City Park) on your left, venue for Johann Strauss and his orchestra and a popular recreational area through the ages. In Edmund Hellmer's **Strauss Monument★**, the gilded figure of the composer (Johann Strauss II) is set against an arch with reliefs of ecstatically writhing Danube nymphs, evidently bewitched by the master's playing.

Leaving **Schwarzenbergplatz★** (KS), with the High Fountain and Russian War Memorial, and then the Hotel Imperial, on the left, you reach the junction of the Ring with Kärntner Strasse, and the **Staatsoper★★** (Opera), built by August von Siccardsburg and Eduard van der Nüll. The Emperor is said to have criticised it slightly, thereby provoking Van der Nüll's suicide and causing Franz Joseph to limit his official remarks thereafter to, 'It is very nice. I liked it very much.'

The next stretch of the boulevard is the **Burgring** (JSHR), flanked to the north-west by the **Burggarten** of the Hofburg and the war memorial and ceremonial gate, the **Burgtor**, leading into the **Heldenplatz★**. On the south-west side is Theophil Hansen's neo-Renaissance **Akademie der Bildenden**

The Schiller statue dominates the park in front of the Academy of Fine Arts; Adolf Hitler failed the entrance exams for the Academy.

Künste★★ (Academy of Fine Arts). This little-visited art collection was originally assembled for didactic purposes, and is also a showcase for the work of former members of the Academy. Its most important painting is the extraordinary **Last Judgement**★★★ (1504) by Hieronymus Bosch. Further along is the **Kunsthistorisches Museum**★★★ (*see* p54) and the **Naturhistorisches Museum**★ (Natural History Museum) (HR). The latter has mineralogical, geological, botanical, zoological, anthropological, prehistorical and speleological departments. The huge collection owes much to the interest of Emperor Franz Stephan in minerals, fossils and shells, which formed the original basis of the museum. The most precious treasure is the 25 000-year-old **Venus of Willendorf**★, a statue of a fertility goddess found in the Wachau some 65km (40

The Naturhistorisches Museum, opened in 1889.

The majestic Pallas Athene fountain in front of Theophil van Hansen's neo-Classical Parliament. Notice too, to the right, the spire of the Rathaus.

Between the two great museum buildings stands the monument to Maria Theresia, which depicts her clasping the Pragmatic Sanction, the symbol of her legitimacy as heir to Charles VI.

miles) up the Danube valley from Vienna.

There is an impressive **monument to Maria Theresia** (1888) in the park that lies inbetween the two museums. Caspar von Zumbusch's design incorporates the ruler on a throne surrounded by her generals and advisers depicted on the plinth, as well as the figures of Gluck, Haydn and Mozart.

Where the Ring turns to the north is the great **Parlament** (HR) by Theophil van Hansen, fronted by Carl Kundmann's **Pallas Athene★** fountain. Opposite is the **Volksgarten★**, with its imitation 'Theseus Temple' and a monument to Empress Elisabeth, the unhappy wife of Franz Joseph, as well as one to Austria's greatest dramatist, Franz Grillparzer. At the western end of the garden is the **Burgtheater★**, considered by many to have the finest traditions in the German-speaking world. The theatre faces Friedrich Schmidt's stupendous neo-Gothic **Rathaus** (City Hall), in front of which are held Christmas fairs, circuses or showings of opera on an open-air screen, according to season. (*Tours of the Rathaus are possible and there is an information centre at the rear entrance.*)

Further west around Schottentor are the 19C and post-war university buildings. Facing across the Ring, opposite Heinrich Ferstel's neo-Renaissance **Universität** (University), is a monument to Andreas Liebenberg, Mayor of Vienna during the 1683 siege. The vast **Votivkirche** (Votive Church) beyond Schottentor is also by Ferstel. The Archduke Maximilian (future Emperor of Mexico), suggested its construction to commemorate his brother,

Illuminated by the lights of the traditional Christmas market, the neo-Gothic Rathaus looks like something out of a fairy-tale.

Franz Joseph's, escape from an assassination attempt by an Hungarian tailor in 1853. It contains a fine Renaissance **tomb★** for Count Salm, defender of Vienna in the siege of 1529.

Schottenring (JP) leads from Schottentor back towards the Danube Canal. On the left are two of Vienna's more distinguished hotels (De France and Vienna Plaza), while the last monument to the Liberal era is Hansen's extremely elegant **Börse** (Stock Exchange) on the south side of the Ring. To the north you will glimpse the striking Italianate **Rossauer Kaserne**, originally built in the 1860s as a huge barracks and munitions depot to keep the citizens in order should they rebel again, and subsequently used by the police departments. A short walk round to the right, along the Franz-Josefs-Kai fronting the canal, leads back to Schwedenplatz.

The first building on the Ringstrasse to be initiated, the Votivkirche, took 23 years to complete, largely because the architect Ferstel was a perfectionist and would only use skilled craftsmen and traditional methods.

EXPLORING VIENNA

KUNSTHISTORISCHES MUSEUM★★★
(MUSEUM OF ART HISTORY)

The picture collection of the museum grew
from that of Archduke Wilhelm of Habsburg
(1614-1662), who was the Governor of the
Netherlands. It was constantly enlarged,
always reflecting the tastes of individual
Habsburg monarchs and Archdukes. The
Kunsthistorisches Museum itself opened in
1891, when the dispersed antiquities of the
dynasty were all brought under one roof. It
was originally intended to be a part of the
huge **Kaiserforum** (Imperial Forum)
glorifying the Habsburgs as promoters of
culture, a megalomaniacal project designed
by Gottfried Semper to link the Hofburg,
across the Ringstrasse, to a vast museums
area. In the event, Semper quarrelled with
his co-architect and only the
Naturhistorisches and Kunsthistorisches
Museums were built. Of the five separate
collections, the paintings should not be
missed, but the visitor should not try to cram
everything into a single visit.

Climb the stairs to the first floor of Karl
Hasenauer's building, noting on the way the
ceiling fresco by Mihály Munkácsy, *The
Apotheosis of the Renaissance*, and the
outstanding stairway lunettes of famous
artists, many of these executed by the
leading artist of the Ringstrassen era, Hans
Makart. The decoration of the cupola space
at the top honours the great Habsburg
collectors.

*The great dome at
the Kunsthistorisches
Museum's entrance
displays the
medallions of the
Habsburg emperors
responsible for the
museum's art
collections.*

The Paintings★★★
Most items come from those areas where the
Habsburgs ruled (North Italy, the

54

Netherlands and Spain). Highlights include Giorgione's **The Three Philosophers★★**, Raphael's celebrated **Madonna of the Meadow★★** (Cabinet 4) and the delightful portraits of the children of the Spanish Habsburg line by Velazquez. The collection of Brueghel in Room X is outstanding and includes **The Tower of Babel★★** as well as three marvellous works from a cycle depicting the seasons. Other highlights of the gallery include **The Adoration of the Holy Trinity★★** by Albrecht Dürer (Cabinet 16), and his **Portrait of Maximilian I★** (Cabinet 17). Nearby is Lucas Cranach's **Judith with the Head of Holofernes★**.

Sculpture and Decorative Arts★★

The most celebrated item is Benvenuto Cellini's gold **salt-cellar★★** (1543) in the form of a reclining Neptune and a nude representing the earth. This is in the Italian Renaissance section, but there are also beautiful artefacts from the German Renaissance, Baroque and Mannerist periods, including some fascinatingly naturalistic busts of Habsburg rulers. French Mannerism, Baroque and medieval art are also well represented, a highlight being a 12C gilded bronze **aquamanile★** encrusted with silver ornament and shaped in the form of a griffon.

Benvenuto Cellini's famous gold salt-cellar, once owned by François I.

The **Egyptian and Near Eastern Collection★★** is rich in sarcophagi, sculpture and jewellery, one of the loveliest objects being a miniature **hippopotamus in blue faience** (2 000 BC) in Room VII. In the **Greek, Etruscan and Roman Collection★★** there are sculptures, bronzes, vases and the superb **Gemma Augustea★★★** – a finely carved onyx cameo (circa AD 12) celebrating the military triumphs of the Emperor Augustus. There are half a million items in the **Coins and Medals Collection**, which is currently closed.

KÄRNTNER STRASSE

The shopping precinct of the Kärntner Strasse (JRS) begins at the Staatsoper in the south-west, behind which is the celebrated **Sacher Hotel**, after whose original owner *Sachertorte* is named. The hotel was built in 1876 for Eduard Sacher, and became famous

Providentia Fountain in Neuer Markt is a copy – Donner's original lead figures are displayed in the Lower Belvedere.

as a place where aristocrats kept assignations with dancers and singers from the adjacent opera.

Almost immediately on the right on the Kärntner Strasse is the 14C **Malteserkirche** (Church of the Knights of St John of Malta),

with a later neo-Classical façade. Inside is a dramatic relief showing Valletta under siege by the Turks in 1558. At No 41 is the delightful Rococo **Esterhazy Palais**, while down Annagasse to the right is the charming little Baroque **Annakirche** (Church of St Anne). From Annagasse, turn left and second left again to reach Himmelpfortgasse and the imposing **Stadtpalais des Prinzen Eugen**★ (Winter Palace of Prince Eugene of Savoy) (KR), in which both Fischer von Erlach and Hildebrandt had a hand. It is now the Ministry of Finance.

Continue back across Kärntner Strasse and bear left into **Neuer Markt** (JR), on which stands a copy of Georg Raphael Donner's **Providentia Fountain**★★ (1739). It was considered indecent by Maria Theresia (or at least by her 'Chastity Commission') and was for a while removed. Providentia presides over allegorical figures representing Austrian rivers (Enns, March, Traun and Ybbs; *see* p21).

At the western corner of the square is the entrance to the **Kapuzinerkirche**★ (Capuchin Church), underneath which lie the vaults of the **Kapuzinergruft**★★ (Imperial Crypt; *see* p60). Here, 143 Habsburgs are laid to rest, the only commoner among them being Maria Theresia's governess. The finest tomb, by Balthasar Moll, was made for Maria Theresia and her husband, Franz Stephan of Lorraine (d.1765). The imperial couple are depicted on the top of the double **tomb**★★, gazing into each other's eyes, while a genius floats above them, bearing a crown of stars. In contrast, the remains of their son, the rationalist Emperor Joseph II, lie in a simple copper coffin in front of the tomb. Franz Joseph I and his assasinated wife, Empress Elisabeth (immortalised in the film 'Sissi'), lie with their son, Rudolf, who committed suicide. The last reigning Habsburg, Empress Zita (1892-1989), is also buried here.

The Capuchin Church above is also worth a visit, particularly the Imperial Chapel which has statues of the Emperors Matthias, Ferdinand II and III and King Ferdinand IV. The fine Baroque *pietà* in the Chapel of the Holy Cross was originally made for the crypt.

If you return to Kärntner Strasse and walk up to the Kärntner Durchgang on the left at the northern end, you will find the famous **American Bar**, designed by Adolf Loos. The recently-restored interior is a symphony of mahogany, marble and brass, all made larger than life by the huge wall mirrors. Loos regarded it as a little bit of American sophistication in the heart of hidebound old Vienna.

The Tomb of Franz Joseph is flanked by his wife Elisabeth and their son Rudolf.

The Death Cult in Vienna

'Death must be a Viennese', runs an ancient saying, and it is true that Vienna has elevated death into a cult, surrounding it with elaborate ritual, and integrating it into many aspects of daily life. Crown Prince Rudolf, who committed suicide at Mayerling in 1889, kept a skull on his desk as a *memento mori*. Indeed, the imperial dynasty set the tone in such matters with a unique necrological cult: the hearts of the deceased Habsburgs were deposited in silver urns in the Loreto Chapel of the Augustinerkirche (whose monks, incidentally, formed a Brotherhood of the Dead responsible for burying the corpses of executed criminals); the embalmed

Habsburg entrails were placed in the catacombs of St Stephen's and the other remains deposited in the Kapuzinergruft. The purpose of this otherwise inexplicably macabre procedure was to create focal points for devotion to the dynasty around the city, an idea that seems to have come from the Spanish branch of the Habsburgs.

Vienna's **Bestattungs-museum** (Burial Museum, *Goldeggasse 19; open by appointment only, weekdays noon-3pm,* ☎ *501 95 227*), one of only a handful in the world, may not be to everyone's taste but gives a good idea of the significance attached to obsequies in the city, which had their origin in the preaching and spectacle of the Counter-Reformation. Joseph II took a coldly rational view of death and burial, as of everything else, and tried to force the people to adopt re-usable coffins, with false bottoms for dropping out the corpses. This idea had to be abandoned, however, when it nearly provoked a riot. In the same museum there is a coffin

Left: Tomb of Karl VI by Balthasar Moll. Right: Detail from a tomb.

fitted with an emergency bell-pull, to alert people on the surface should you have been buried alive (not absolutely improbable, given the limitations of contemporary medical diagnosis). In order to avoid such a disagreeable fate, you could give orders that your corpse was to be stabbed through the heart before burial.

Viennese cortèges were magnificent affairs, and even the cheapest had accompanying musicians. However Karl Lueger, mayor from 1897 to 1910, having the interests of the poorer folk at heart, put a stop to profiteering by undertakers with the introduction of municipal funerals at fixed prices.

Hermann Bahr, the turn-of-the-century critic and writer, caught the attitude of the city's inhabitants very well when he wrote: 'He who would understand how a Viennese lives must know how he is buried; for his being is deeply bound up with his no-longer-being, about which he is constantly singing bitter-sweet songs.'

Across the Kärntner Strasse from here, the Weihburggasse leads down past the **Drei Husaren** (one of Vienna's most distinguished old-style restaurants) to the Franciscan square and **Franziskanerkirche** (KR). The Franciscans took over the city's home for fallen women in 1589 and built their cloister and church on the site. The interior decoration of the church has striking Baroque illusionist effects typical of the age.

The Kärntner Strasse itself has many of Vienna's most fashionable shops, including that of **Lobmeyr glass**, with its marvellous Historicist and Jugendstil designs. **Backhausen** sells fabrics in patterns of the Wiener Werkstätte, and a shop adjacent to St Stephen's (actually on Stock-im-Eisen-Platz) sells the home-produced **Augarten pottery**. There is also a good bookshop (Georg Prachner), a music shop and several congenial cafés overlooking the busy pedestrian zone.

AROUND FLEISCHMARKT

(*The north-eastern part of the Inner City is a short walk from traffic connections at either Schwedenplatz or Stephansdom.*) Walking east along the Fleischmarkt (KR), the old meat market, you soon reach on the left the **Griechenbeisl**, which is the successor to an ancient inn where the legendary bagpiper, Augustin, entertained customers during the plague year of 1679. He fell into a pit of plague corpses when returning home drunk, but survived to be celebrated in a famous song '*O du lieber Augustin*'. The narrow Griechengasse leads down to a small church given by Maria Theresia in 1776 for the use of Greeks still under Ottoman rule.

At Fleischmarkt 13, however, is the striking **Griechische Kirche** (Greek Orthodox Trinity Church), financed by a 19C banker of Greek origin and built by Theophil Hansen in the 1860s. It boasts a fine iconostasis.

Passing the redeveloped Central Post Office at Fleischmarkt 19, which now has a telecommunications shopping mall, veer right into Postgasse past the diminutive **Uniat Church of St Barbara** at No 10. The Uniat churches were orthodox in certain respects but in communion with Rome.

Turning into Postgasse is the **Dominikanerkirche** (Dominican Church), built in 1634 on the site of two earlier sanctuaries. It is dedicated to the Rosary

Inspired by Byzantine architecture, Theophil Hansen adorned the Griechische Kirche with lavish gold embellishment.

Madonna, St Dominic having supposedly
invented the prayer cycle of the rosary in the
course of his battle against the Albigensian
heresy. Inside is a statue of him as a wandering
preacher, his faithful dog beside him.

A right turn off Postgasse brings you into
Dr.-Ignaz-Seipel-Platz (KR 27), named after
the inter-war Chancellor of Austria, who was
also a Catholic priest. To the south-east is the
Alte Universität (Old University), which the
Jesuits gained control of (1622) as part of
the Habsburg Counter-Reformatory drive.
They built their **church★** just to the north-
east of the university in 1631. Below the
upper row of sculptured saints of its façade
you will see the figures of St Ignatius and
Francis Xavier, co-founders of the Jesuit
order. The Baroque interior, with curlicue
columns, has a fine cycle of frescoes
representing *The Life of Mary, The Fall of the*

*The relatively
restrained façade of
the Jesuit Church
belies the
extravagant
Baroque interior.*

Angels, and *The Trinity.* On the south side of the square is the elegant **Akademie der Wissenschaften** (Academy of Sciences, 1755), originally the aula of the university until the Academy was founded under Metternich. It is now used for bestowing university degrees and for symposia.

If you leave the square by the Sonnenfelsgasse and then turn right into Schönlaterngasse (KR 100), you come to a gate leading into the spacious and peaceful courtyard of the **Heiligenkreuzerhof**, the city base of the Cistercian monks of Heiligenkreuz. The prelacy is used for exhibitions by the High School of Applied Art, and the large residential block is let as flats which have traditionally been favoured by artists and writers.

Leaving the Heiligenkreuzerhof at the north-west end, turn left into Köllnerhofgasse and into Bäckerstraße (KR 9), from which there is a passageway running south towards Wollzeile. Here is the famous *Figlmüller* restaurant, which supplies the biggest and best Wiener Schnitzel in Vienna, served by waiters who are renowned for their typically Wienerisch *Schlagfertigkeit* (repartee).

Enjoying the famous Wiener Schnitzel in the Figlmüller restaurant.

JUDENPLATZ – AM HOF – FREYUNG★

The earliest Jewish community was under the protection of the Babenbergs and its dwellings thus clustered next to the ducal palace **Am Hof**. As church-inspired anti-Semitism grew, the area (today's **Judenplatz**) (JR 67) gradually became a ghetto, much of it being destroyed in the pogrom of 1421. In 1935 a monument to Gotthold Lessing, author of *Nathan the Wise*, the hero of which was a wise, conciliating Jew, was erected on the square but later removed by the Nazis. It was reinstated in 1968. A controversial holocaust monument by the British sculptress, Rachel Whiteread, is now nearing completion and is due to be in place by 1998, unless objections raised prevent this.

Copper and gold ornamentation predominate on the Jugendstil Ankeruhr.

On the north side of the square is the former **Böhmische Hofkanzlei** (Bohemian Chancellery, 1714) by Fischer von Erlach, on which you can see the coats of arms of Bohemia, Silesia and Moravia. In the street beyond is the **Altes Rathaus** (Old City Hall) at Wipplingerstrasse 8, containing the Museum of the Inner City and that of the Austrian Resistance Movement during the Second World War. At the rear is a fine Renaissance door to the late-13C **Salvatorkapelle**. The same street runs east to the **Hoher Markt** (KR) where a major attraction is the Jugendstil **Ankeruhr** (Clock of the Anchor Insurance Company), placed on a bridging buttress between their two buildings. At noon, 12 figures from Viennese history rotate around the clockface. Wipplingerstrasse, in the other

The delicate filigree spire of the lovely Maria am Gestade reflects the evening sun.

direction from the Altes Rathaus, leads to
Schwertgasse on the right, which in turn
takes you to one of the loveliest churches in
Vienna, the Gothic **Maria am Gestade★**
(Mary on the River Bank). It is so-called
because the Danube still washed the bank
below it when it was built by Michael Knab in
the late 14C.

Striking south-west from Judenplatz
through the narrow Schulhof (JR 105), you
pass the **Uhrenmuseum der Stadt Wien★**
(Clock Museum). This is an absolutely
delightful place to linger, being situated on
three storeys of a small Inner City palace
that once belonged to Count Starhemberg,
Vienna's garrison commander during the
siege of 1683. There is a wide assortment of
picture-clocks, novelty items and
astronomical clocks (one of the last named
has a pointer requiring 20 904 years for a
complete revolution!). Just next door at
Schulhof 4 is the **Puppen- und
Spielzeugmuseum** (Doll and Toy Museum),
which has some impressive dolls' houses, as
well as teddy bears and a large number of
mostly French and German dolls.

Moving on through the Schulhof, you
emerge next to the **Kirche zu den neun
Chören der Engel** (Jesuit Church of the
Nine Choirs of Angels). From the balcony of
this church, a herald announced the
Habsburgs' abandonment of their claim to
the title of Holy Roman Emperor, in 1806.
Across the square is the former **Zeughaus**
(Citizens' Armoury, 1732) with roof
sculpture by Lorenzo Mattielli representing
Strength and Courage holding up a gilded
globe. In the centre of Am Hof is the
Immaculata Monument, originally erected
under Ferdinand III after a Swedish army

*The delightful
Freyung – on the
left is the Harrach
Palace and the
recently restored
Schottenkirche is in
the centre.*

failed to take Vienna (1645) during the Thirty Years' War. The present column is a later copy put up by Leopold I.

To the north-west of Am Hof is the area known as **Freyung★**, a reference to the asylum available to fugitives from the law in the precincts of the **Schottenstift★** (Monastery of the Scots), on the north side, a right that lasted until the time of Joseph II (1782). The 'Scots' Benedictine convent (actually the monks were Irish) was founded in 1155 under Heinrich II of Babenberg, who moved his residence to neighbouring Am Hof the following year. The Benedictines' church, **Schottenkirche**, (recently restored) has a huge neo-Renaissance altar (1883) designed by the Ringstrassen architect, Heinrich Ferstel. Other points of interest are Fischer von

Erlach's sarcophagus for Count
Starhemberg, and the Babenberg crypt. The
Schottenhof, behind the church, contains a
museum with the celebrated
Schottenaltar★★, a late-Gothic winged altar
by a local master which has the first painted
scenes of Vienna in the background.

To the north-west are
some distinguished
Baroque palaces, notably
the **Palais Kinsky** (1716) at
No 4, by Lukas von
Hildebrandt. On the south-
west corner is the imposing
Palais Harrach, now used
for exhibitions by the
Kunsthistorisches Museum,
but well worth visiting in its
own right for its
magnificently restored
interiors (for instance, the
superb marble stairway).
Adjoining it is the Freyung
entrance to the so-called
Palais Ferstel (1860), in fact
a triangular site on which
Heinrich Ferstel designed a
building for multiple use
(the Austro-Hungarian

*The Danube
Fountain (1861)
stands at the end of
the arcade running
through the Ferstel
Palace.*

Bank, the Stock Exchange, fashionable
shops and the famous Café Central, which
still occupies the ground floor). The last-
named was a favourite haunt of Viennese
literati at the turn of the century, described
by one of them as 'a place for people who
want to be alone, but who need company to
be alone in'. In the glass-covered arcade that
runs through the middle of the Palais Ferstel
there is a pleasant restaurant, and at its
south-west end, the pretty **Danube Fountain**.

KARLSPLATZ★★

Just outside the Kärntner Ring is the heart of Viennese music, the **Musikvereinsge-bäude** (Concert Hall of the Society of the Friends of Music), a splendidly ornate building by Theophil Hansen and the venue for the famous New Year's Day Concert of the Wiener Philharmoniker.

South of the Musikverein (reached by an underpass) is **Karlsplatz★★** (JKS), with the **Historisches Museum der Stadt Wien★** (Historical Museum of the City of Vienna) at its eastern end. The collection has artefacts from every period of Viennese history, from the Hallstatt culture (9C-5C BC) up to the early 20C. Highlights include a plan and a maquette of Vienna made respectively in 1548 and the 1850s, paintings by artists of the Secession and the Austrian Expressionists, and a reconstruction of Adolf Loos's sitting room, which looks remarkably English.

Beyond the museum rises the lovely **Karlskirche★★** (Church of St Carlo Borromeo), the greatest work by Fischer von Erlach, father and son. Karl VI built it in thanksgiving for deliverance from the last great plague to strike Vienna in 1713, in dedication to the plague saint, Carlo Borromeo.

Its most striking features are the two huge columns (modelled on Trajan's column in Rome) that stand in front of the façade, and are covered with a spiralling frieze depicting the life and work of Carlo Borromeo. Above the Classical portico of the church itself, note the statue of an angel withdrawing his sword from the city, symbolic of the ending of the plague.

The Vienna Secession

In 1897 a group of Viennese artists, frustrated by the conservative policies of the official Künstlerhaus, seceded from that organisation and set up their own. Their leader was **Gustav Klimt**, who had begun his career as a brilliant executor of the required society painting, an example of which is his picture of the Burgtheater audience, containing exact portraits of hundreds of local worthies. Increasingly, however, he became aware of the sterility of this artistic milieu and was attracted by the new foreign trends such as Art Nouveau and Symbolism. Forming an alliance with **Otto Wagner**, an officially respected city architect (who designed the famous Karlsplatz pavilions for Vienna's new rapid transit railway), Klimt and his colleagues persuaded the industrialist Karl Wittgenstein to finance a new exhibition hall for a site audaciously and provocatively situated just behind the Academy of Fine

Arts. Both the design of the Secession building (which incorporated the modern idea of movable partitions) and the nature of the shows (which for the first time included avant-garde artists from abroad) were something completely novel for Vienna, but met with astonishingly rapid success.

The Secession was above all a Viennese phenomenon, although **Josef Hoffmann** and **Kolo Moser** produced artefacts and furniture, and even complete interiors, that owe a lot to the ideas of the famous Scottish designer, Charles Rennie Mackintosh, and the Englishman associated with the Arts and Crafts Movement, C R Ashbee. Their style (*Würfelstil*) was characterised by black and white diaper patterns, puritanical and strongly geometric in contrast to the emotional flowing lines of mainstream Art Nouveau. The architect Otto Wagner's style was also *sui generis*, although owing something to Jugendstil (as Art Nouveau was called in Central Europe). His attention to functional appropriateness, and his incorporation of functional aspects as visible features of a building's design, made him a precursor of Modernism (see his Post Office Savings Bank, and his church for the Lower Austrian Clinic for Nervous Diseases am Steinhof).

The pictures by Klimt, **Carl Moll** and other members of the Secession may be seen in the Austrian Art Gallery of the Belvedere. Klimt's beautiful, symbolic gold paintings, such as *The Kiss* or *Judith*, were influenced by the Byzantine mosaics that he saw in Ravenna on one of his rare trips abroad. His landscapes with flattened perspectives (partly influenced by Japanese prints) are among the finest works of the turn of the century in Europe.

Left: Secession Building.
Below: Gustav Klimt's The Kiss.

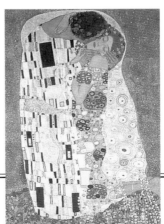

In the **cupola★★** of the interior, Johann
Michael Rottmayr's fresco depicts Carlo
Borromeo's *Intercession with the Almighty* for
his afflicted people, with the Virgin Mary
lending her support. In front of the church
is a shallow pool, in the centre of which is
Henry Moore's sculpture of *Hill Arches*,
donated by the sculptor when the square was
being remodelled in 1978.

If you continue west, leaving the old and
new Technical Universities on your left, as
well as Hansen's attractive **Lutheran School**
(Karlsplatz 14), you come to the graceless
new **Kunsthalle** (Exhibition Hall). Beyond it

*The Baroque
masterpiece,
Karlskirche, is
flanked by twin
columns inspired by
Trajan's Column in
Rome.*

you will see the recently restored white walls of the **Secessionsgebäude★★** (Secession building). Financed by the industrialist Karl Wittgenstein (father of the philosopher), it was designed by Joseph Maria Olbrich as the first exhibition hall for the artists of the Vienna Secession (*see* p72). Gustav Klimt's **Beethoven Frieze★★★** is on display inside the building, a homage to the composer made for an exhibition dedicated to Beethoven in 1902. The frieze is a visual representation of the themes of the Ninth Symphony and the final panel shows two quotations from Schiller's *Ode to Joy*.

SCHLOSS BELVEDERE★★

The **Unteres Belvedere★** (Lower Belvedere) is entered from Rennweg 6A (KS) and houses the **Österreichisches Barockmuseum★★** (Austrian Baroque Museum). Highlights

The Lower Belvedere, seen from the Lower Cascade in the splendid gardens.

Detail from the façade of the Upper Belvedere.

The approach to the magnificent Baroque Upper Belvedere is through the colourful formal gardens laid out by Dominique Girard.

include the works by Georg Raphael Donner (including his original lead figures for the **Providentia Fountain★★** on the Neuer Markt; *see* p57). Unique are the extraordinary grimacing **faces★★** by Franz Xaver Messerschmidt. In the adjacent orangery is the **Museum Mittelalterlicher Österreichischer Kunst★** (Museum of Austrian Medieval Art). This contains some superb Gothic works of the 14C and 15C, including stone figures by the Master of Grosslobming and important works by the Tyrolean master, Michael Pacher.

The Lower Belvedere was the business end of Prince Eugene of Savoy's great palace, built with the rewards he received for his success in the Turkish Wars and fighting the French in the Netherlands. In the **cabinet doré★★** is a Baroque celebration of the owner, Balthasar Permoser's *Apotheosis of Prince Eugene* (1721), while in the spectacular marble hall is Martino Altomonte's similarly flattering fresco showing another apotheosis, with the Prince here being identified with the sun-god Apollo.

Leaving the Lower Belvedere, walk through the fine park laid out by Dominique Girard, which rises towards the **Oberes Belvedere★★** (Upper Belvedere) and originally had sculptural decoration praising the dual nature of Prince Eugene as a man of culture (Apollo) and a man of war (Hercules).

The Prince's architect, Lukas von Hildebrandt, began work on the Belvedere in 1714, completing the lower part in 1716 and the glorious upper palace in 1722. The largest and noblest aristocratic palace in Central Europe now houses the **Österreichische Galerie★★** (Austrian Art

Gallery), containing exclusively Austrian works from the 19C onwards, except for some foreign pictures of the same period recently transferred when the Neue Galerie in the Hofburg was dissolved. The Austrian works include masterpieces by the leading painters of Historicism (Hans Makart, V*enice Welcomes Catherina Cornaro*), domestic portraiture and landscapes of the Biedermeier bourgeoisie from the first half of the 19C, and mid-century Realist painting. The most celebrated works, however, are those by Gustav Klimt (**The Kiss★★★** (*see* p73) and *Allee in the Park at Schloss Kammer*), and the other Secessionists, notably Carl Moll. Another magnet for visitors is the work of the Austrian Expressionists such as Egon Schiele (**Death and the Maiden★★**, **The Family★**) and Oskar Kokoschka (**The Tiger-Lion★**).

Before leaving the palace, visit the **Festsaal** on the first floor, the ceiling fresco of which is another tribute to Prince Eugene (*Fame and Glory* by Carlo Carlone). It was here that the *Staatsvertrag*, liberating Austria from allied occupation in 1955, was signed. A contemporary picture shows the assembled Foreign Ministers: Dulles, Macmillan, Pinay, Molotov and Leopold Figl (for Austria).

Around Schloss Belvedere

Leave the Upper Belvedere via Prinz-Eugen-Strasse and turn right to approach the Baroque Schwarzenberg Palace (1720), now a luxury hotel and restaurant. A left turn takes you up to the **Gürtel** (Outer Ring Road), across which is the **Schweizer Garten** and the **Museum des 20 Jahrhunderts** (Museum of the Twentieth Century), the latter a venue for modern art shows. Further

Schloss Schönbrunn, the former imperial summer residence, took its name from the beautiful spring on the site of the palace.

east through the park is the great **Arsenal**, a complex of 19C military buildings once including a barracks, a hospital, a chapel, a gunnery school, and still housing the **Heeresgeschichtliches Museum**★ (War Museum). This is worth a visit: there is a hall of fame with busts of Austrian military heroes and a chronological survey of warfare in Austrian history, beginning with the Turkish siege of 1683 and ending with the First World War.

SCHLOSS SCHÖNBRUNN★★★
(SCHÖNBRUNN PALACE)

The original plans for enlarging Schloss Schönbrunn (AZ) from a hunting lodge, purchased by Maximilian I, were drawn up by Johann Bernhard Fischer von Erlach.

They envisaged a Versailles-like edifice on the top of the hill where the Gloriette now stands. The final scaled-down version (1749) on the plain below is the work of Maria Theresia's architect, Nikolaus Pacassi, and was designed as a summer retreat in Rococo style. The yellow ochre of its walls was to become standard for all public buildings in the Austrian Empire and Schönbrunn became a focal point of the dynasty (Franz Joseph was born and died there after a rule of 68 years, and his successor abdicated in a room within the palace).

Near the main entrance to the right is the **Schlosstheater** (*summer opera programmes*), with a fine neo-Classical interior by Ferdinand von Hohenberg, who also designed the **Gloriette★★** (1773) above the park on the south side, and the artificial

Set on a hill behind the palace, the neo-Classical arcade of the Gloriette has superb views across the formal gardens to Schönbrunn and to the city beyond.

Roman ruins, also in the gardens to the south. The latter were a romantic folly symbolising the destruction of the enemies of the Empire, while the former, a colonnaded triumphal arch, celebrated Maria Theresia's victories over Frederick the Great of Prussia. The **view** from the Gloriette is superb, and there is a pleasant small café under the arcade.

There are two **tours** of the interior of Schloss Schönbrunn, the comprehensive **Grand Tour** of 40 rooms (out of a possible 1 441!), and the **Imperial Tour**, which takes in 22 rooms. The areas of particular historic or aesthetic interest are as follows: **Franz Joseph's bedroom and study**, with the Emperor's ascetic iron bedstead; the **Mirror Gallery**, where in 1762 the infant prodigy Mozart performed for Maria Theresia and her family; the two **Chinese Rooms** with Oriental porcelain and gilt panelling featuring Chinese-style landscapes, a reflection of the Rococo taste for 'Chinoiserie'; the **Great Gallery★★★** and **Small Gallery**, both with frescoes by Guglielmo Guglielmi. The **Blue Chinese Salon★** is where Karl I abdicated in 1918; the **Vieux-Lacque Zimmer★** features Japanese-style landscapes; the **Millionenzimmer★** (so-called because of its cost), has rosewood panelling with Indian and Persian miniatures; and lastly, a room of some pathos is dedicated to the Duc de Reichstadt, Napoleon's son by Marie Louise of Austria, daughter of Franz I. He died young and you can see his death mask here, together with a pet lark that he had stuffed on its demise, the companion of a boyhood passed in the semi-incarceration of Schönbrunn.

The Park★★

In the woodland to the south-east of the palace is the original 'beautiful spring' from which Schönbrunn takes its name: there is a grotto (1771) by Isidore Canevale and a statue of a nymph (Wilhelm Beyer, 1779) pouring the spring water from a pitcher. The central gravel path leads south towards Wilhelm Beyer's **Neptune Fountain** (1781), above which rises the Gloriette. To the west is a glass and iron **Palmenhaus★** (Palm House, 1882), which rivals those at Kew Gardens, London, in size and magnificence, and the **Botanische Garten** (Botanical Garden). Bordering Hietzing in the west is the **Tiergarten★** (zoo), which has a long history going back to Maximilian I's menagerie on a site near today's Central Cemetery. The **octagonal pavilion** inside was used by the imperial family in the 18C for viewing the animals and now houses a café.

The huge Palm House is home to an impressive collection of exotic and tropical plants.

AROUND THE SERVITENKIRCHE
(SERVITE CHURCH)

A short walk up Währinger Strasse from
Schottentor brings you past the entrance to
Strudelhofgasse on the right, at the end of
which is Theodor Jäger's Art Nouveau flight
of steps, **Strudlhofstiege**, 1910. Descending
these, you arrive shortly at the great
Liechtenstein Palais (*Fürstengasse 1*),
completed in 1711 by Domenico Martinelli.
Apart from the interesting features of the
building itself, (the **sala terrena** with
medallions by J M Rottmayr, and the
Prunksaal with Andrea Pozzo's ceiling fresco
of *The Apotheosis of Hercules*), the palace is still
home to the **Museum Moderner Kunst**
(Museum of Modern Art). Temporary
exhibitions are held on the first floor, while
on the second the permanent collection
includes works by Cubists, Futurists,
Surrealists and Pop artists.

A walk via Fürstengasse, Porzellangasse
and Grünentorgasse brings you to the
Servitenkirche (Servite Church, 1679) by
Carlo Canevale, the first Viennese church to
be based on an oval ground-plan. In the
chapels under the towers at the entrance are
two superb stucco lustro chapels by Giovanni
Bussi and Giovanni Barbarina. They
represent in vivid narrative scenes *The
Martyrdom of St John Nepomuk* and *The Death
of St Juliana Falconieri* (founder of the Servite
order of nuns). The **pulpit★** is also
remarkable, with its carved figures by
Balthasar Moll of the Four Evangelists and
the Three Virtues, and the church also
boasts an exquisite 15C *pietà*. The Peregrini
Chapel (extending the middle chapel on the
right) has some beautiful Rococo ironwork

and frescoes by Josef Mölk.

The Servitengasse heads south to the Berggasse, at No 19 of which is the **Sigmund-Freud-Museum**★ (*open 9am-4pm*), housed in Freud's former consulting rooms and his home from 1891 until he was forced to flee Austria by the Nazis. The vestibule and rooms preserve the domestic atmosphere of the Freud home and there are also some of his antiquities on display, but the famous couch remains in London.

PRATER★

An example of the outstanding stucco in the Servitenkirche; this section depicts a scene from the life of St John Nepomuk.

The huge area (3 200 acres) of the Prater (CY) was originally an imperial hunting ground, opened to the public by the enlightened Emperor Joseph II in 1766. In the 19C there was a flower parade of society notables along the (5km/3 mile) chestnut allée each spring – the *Blumenkorso*. Here, the annual May Day march of workers was held for the first time in 1890, and thereafter became an annual event.

Apart from opportunities for riding, walking and jogging, the main attractions of the park (especially in the evening) are in the sector known as the **Wurstelprater**. In and around this part is a vast funfair, featuring Calafati's famous roundabout (1840) guarded by the 'Great Chinaman'. Apart from the dodgems, miniature railway, big dipper, ghost train, shooting galleries and the like, there are also men on stilts, sword-swallowers, magicians, pony rides and other attractions for children of all ages. In addition, there are innumerable small booths and eateries offering snack food and local specialities.

Dominating the whole area is the great **Riesenrad★★** (Ferris Wheel) some 64.7m (212ft) high, built by the Englishman Walter Basset in 1897. It offers magnificent **views** of the city from the top of its rotation. Aficionados of the film classic *The Third Man* will recall that Harry Lime contemplated hurling his naive friend to his death as their cabin reached the top. The **Planetarium** is situated in the main avenue and also contains a history of the Prater (*open weekends, 2-4.30pm, not August*).

OTHER ATTRACTIONS

Outside the Inner City (First District) of Vienna, there are a number of other places well worth visiting. In the Second District is the extensive **Augarten** (CY) (*Bus 5A from Nestroyplatz*), with the porcelain factory of the same name and the college of the Vienna Boys Choir. Joseph II opened the park to the public, and a triumphal arch over the entrance on Obere Augartenstrasse has a dedicatory inscription to his people by the Emperor.

In the Third District is the post-modern **Hundertwasserhaus** (*corner Löwengasse/ Kegelgasse, Tram N from Schwedenplatz*), a multi-coloured extravaganza draped with greenery. The idea behind this work (commissioned by the City of Vienna in 1985) is partly ecological, Hundertwasser seeing the abundantly integrated greenery of the balconies as 'ambassadors of the forest in the city'.

In the Eighth District (*Josefstadt, Tram J*) is the fine **Piaristenkirche Basilika Maria Treu** (Church of Maria Treu, 1751), with a convex façade by Kilian Ignaz Dientzenhofer of Prague and superb frescoes of biblical scenes inside by Franz Anton Maulbertsch.

A longer trek is required to visit the **Geymüller-Schlössl** at Khevenhüllerstrasse 2 (*Tram 41 to the end stop, then a short walk*).

The Hundertwasserhaus is a municipal apartment block, the design of which aimed to alleviate the monotony of modern city architecture.

This is a charming Romantic villa built around 1808 for a Viennese banker, which contains a **museum** of Empire and Biedermeier furniture and some 160 clocks, mostly 18C. (*Opening times, with a guided tour are limited: Mar-Nov, Tue, Wed, Fri-Sun 10am-3pm.*)

Otto Wagner's **Kirche am Steinhof★★** (AYZ) (*Bus 48A to Baumgartner Höhe*) requires a Saturday afternoon appointment as it is part of a psychiatric clinic (*3-5pm.* ☎ *94 90 60 Ext: 2391*). However, it is well worth taking the trouble, the church being one of Wagner's most memorable works. The ingeniously planned functional interior incorporates safety factors for the inmates, while the decorative élan of the **Secessionist stained glass★** by Kolo Moser and mosaics by Remigius Geyling is no less impressive. The exterior combines monumental gravitas (in the two over-life-size figures of St Severin and St Leopold above the façade) with the Baroque elegance of a mighty dome.

Another church worth visiting is the sculptor Fritz Wotruba's only realised building, the strange **Wotrubakirche** (*in the suburb of Mauer at Georgsgasse/Rysergasse, Bus 60A from Liesing*). Completed in 1975, this ultra-modern building consists of 152 concrete blocks piled up in an asymmetrical pattern (although from certain angles it looks a bit like a telescoped version of Stonehenge). The idea behind the design was that the church should be seen as a force for harmony that overcomes opposing forces.

The **Hermesvilla** (a gift from Franz Joseph to his wife, though she seldom occupied it) is situated in the **Lainzer Tiergarten★** (Wildlife Park – *Tram 60 to Speising, then Bus*

The Wotrubakirche, constructed from huge blocks of concrete, represents an outstanding example of modern architecture by Fritz Wotruba.

60B to the park entrance). In the ten square miles of park, deer, moufflon and wild boar are preserved, these being the ancient indigenous inhabitants of the Wienerwald and the Alps. The Hubertuswarte observation gallery affords a chance to observe them in their natural setting. The villa (1884, by Karl Hasenauer) may be visited and frequently has exhibitions of local historical interest.

The **Zentralfriedhof** (Central Cemetery – *Tram 71 from Schwarzenbergplatz to Simmeringer Hauptstrasse*) is a less depressing excursion than it might sound. Among its three million graves are those of the greatest Viennese. There are separate areas for the non-Catholic faiths represented in Vienna's long cosmopolitan history – Judaism, Islam, Orthodoxy and Protestantism.

OTHER MUSEUMS AND GALLERIES

Vienna is especially rich in museums, many of them unusual and one or two bizarre. The following are worth including on the itinerary, if time permits. (*Note that most museums are open from Tuesday to Sunday, from 9/10am-5/6pm.*)

The **Museum für Österreichische Volkskunde** (Austrian Folklore Museum, *Laudongasse 17-19*) is housed in a fine palace designed for the Schönborn family in 1714. The delightful collection in the recently refurbished display includes all manner of artefacts and functional objects of folk art, from a ceramic stove in the shape of a peasant woman to a carved chess set and votive paintings.

The **Museum für Völkerkunde★** (Ethnology Museum, *in the Neue Hofburg*) is devoted to non-European cultures, in particular to Africa, Japan, and Captain Cook's collection from Oceania.

In the arcade at Hoher Markt 3, in the Inner City, is the entrance to the subterranean ruins of **Roman officers' houses**.

A new museum devoted to the **Lipizzaners** has opened on the edge of the Stallburg. You can also see the horses in their stalls through a window.

Also in the Inner City are the **Neidhart-Fresken** (Neidhart Frescoes, *Tuchlauben 19*), a 15C cycle of wall paintings showing motifs from the poetry of the Minnesänger Neidhart von Reuental.

Near Schönbrunn, the **Technisches Museum** (AZ) (Museum of Technology, *Mariahilfer Strasse 212*) should soon re-open after long closure for restoration (☎ *914 16 10 or 894 01 49 before you visit to confirm*). It contains displays of transport, industry and mining through the ages, as well as a number of Austrian inventions. Historic transport buffs will enjoy the **Strassenbahn-Museum**★ (CY 30) (Tramway Museum, *Erdbergstrasse 109*), which is open at weekends and on public holidays. The **Österreichisches Tabakmuseum** (Tobacco Museum, *Mariahilfer Strasse 2*) is more interesting than it sounds and has some ornate pipes on show, together with displays relating to the history of the tobacco monopoly in Austria.

A bizarre sight is the collection of wax figures used for training military surgeons in dissection, which can be seen in the **Josephinum**★ (*Währinger Strasse 25/1; the Medical Museum is open Mon-Fri 9am-3pm*).

Not far away in the grounds of the **Allgemeines Krankenhaus** (General Hospital) is the so-called **Narrenturm** (Lunatics' Tower), another foundation of Joseph II, originally designed for confining the mentally ill. The cylindrical tower (*entrance via General Hospital at Spitalgasse 2; open Wed 3-6pm, Thur 8-11am*) now contains an extraordinary collection of medical curiosities.

Some **memorial rooms** of artists, writers and composers are of more than passing interest. (*Note that most of them have a lunch break from noon-1pm and close at 4.30pm.*) There are several devoted to Beethoven, who moved house over 30 times during his long stay in the city. The most interesting is **Beethoven-Haus** (BX) (*Probusgasse 6, in Heiligenstadt*), where the famous *Heiligenstädter Testament* is preserved, a moving document written by the composer at the time he began to lose his hearing. The **Pasqualatihaus**★ (*Mölker Bastei 8*) contains memorial rooms not only to Beethoven, but also to the great Austrian novelist of the early 19C, Adalbert Stifter. The **Haydn-Museum**★ (*Haydngasse 19*) also includes a room devoted to the life and work of Johannes Brahms. The **Figaro-Haus**★ (*Domgasse 5*) is where Mozart wrote most of the music for *The Marriage of Figaro*. The **Schubert's Geburtshaus**★ (*Nussdorferstrasse 54*), where he was born, has memorial rooms, while his **death chamber** may be viewed at Kettenbrückengasse 6. The **Lehár-Schlössl** (*Hackhofergasse 18; open March-Nov for groups of five or more;* ☎ *318 54 16*) has memorials of the great operetta composer, Franz Lehár, and of Mozart's librettist on *The Magic Flute*, Emanuel Schikaneder.

Finally, the **Österreichisches Theatermuseum** (Austrian Theatre Museum) has two sections situated close to each other: the main one is in the lovely **Lobkowitz Palais** (*Lobkowitzplatz 2, see* p40) and is worth a visit for the palace's fine interior, quite apart from the exhibits, while the **Memorial Rooms of the Austrian Theatre** feature mementoes of leading 19C and 20C figures from the theatre and operetta (*Hanuschgasse 3; if still under restoration, visits may be possible by appointment;* ☎ *512 24 27*).

EXCURSIONS FROM VIENNA

Heurigen Villages
Around the periphery of the city are numerous attractive wine villages, the most famous of which is **Grinzing**★ (BX) to the north-west (*Tram 38 from Schottentor*). After

the area was destroyed by the Turks, a pretty village grew up in the 18C and 19C. **Heurigen** are taverns that sell the young wine (*Heuriger*) of the current vintage only (theoretically they are supposed to close when supplies are exhausted, but nowadays most of them operate all year round on a commercial basis). Open Heurigen are indicated as '*ausg'steckt*' (i.e. with pine twigs hung over the door). The true Heurigen wine is the so-called *gemischter Satz*, which is a blend of local grape varieties. Simple food is served (the custom of bringing your own is dying out except in a few small inns).

The pretty village of Grinzing, with its charming streets and attractive houses, offers a relaxed escape from the bustle of the city.

As charming as Grinzing is **Heiligenstadt**★ (BX) (*U4, U6 to the end stop, then two stops on Bus 38A*), where Beethoven lived from time to time. There is an ancient parish **church** that once contained the remains of Saint Severin, the Christianised Roman who, according to legend, converted the natives of the Danube Valley. Situated in another former Beethoven residence is one of the

best Heurigen, **Mayer am Pfarrplatz** (next to the church).

There are Heurigen villages to the north, west and south of Vienna, and details of taverns that are *ausg'steckt* may be found in the local press.

Kahlenberg★ and Leopoldsberg★★
(*U4, U6 to Heiligenstadt, then Bus 38A from the U-Bahn station.*) The Höhenstrasse was built under the clerico-Fascist regime of the 1930s to provide access for ramblers to the **Wienerwald** (Vienna Woods) (AXY). The two hills at the eastern end of the Wienerwald were inhabited in prehistoric times. The **Leopoldkirche**, on the **Leopoldsberg★★** (BX) (both names are references to St Leopold of Babenberg), contains a display about the Turkish siege of 1683. It was from these heights that the imperial armies of Christendom swept down to slaughter the besieging Turks. The church of **St Joseph**, on the **Kahlenberg★**, slightly to the east, is the site of the last mass held before the attack, at which the Papal Legate, Marco d' Aviano officiated before King John Sobieski of Poland, the nominal Commander-in-Chief of the army. The semi-circular Kahlenberg-Restaurant has fine **views★** of Vienna.

Klosterneuburg★
(*Reached quickly by the U-Bahn from Franz-Josefs-Bahnhof.*) The monastery and church of Klosterneuburg were founded by St Leopold III of Babenberg at the end of the 12C. Under the Habsburg Karl VI, an ambitious plan of alteration and extension was undertaken by Donato Felice d'Allio, but never completed. The greatest treasure of

the Augustinian monastery is the **wing altar★★** (1191) by Nicholas of Verdun, which may be seen in the cloister. It consists of 51 copper and enamel plaques showing scenes from the Old and New Testaments. In the Stiftskeller of Klosterneuburg is a celebrated 560 hectolitre wine barrel, used as a slide for visitors once a year when the nameday of St Leopold is celebrated. To visit the treasures you must join a tour (*daily 9.30-11am and 1.30-5pm*).

Schloss Laxenburg

(*The three castles here are open from Easter to the end of October and may be reached by train from Wien Mitte to Laxenburg-Biedermannsdorf.*)
The original castle, **Altes Schloss**, was used as a summer residence by the Habsburgs and it was here that Karl VI promulgated his famous *Pragmatic Sanction*, making the

The garden at Schloss Laxenburg, with its hidden grottoes, lake and bridges, has a peaceful and romantic atmosphere.

female line (Maria Theresia) eligible to inherit the dynasty's various thrones and titles. Maria Theresia herself frequently resided in the Baroque **Neues Schloss** (also known as the Blauer Hof), which later became the venue for sessions of the Congress of Vienna (1814-15) after the Napoleonic War. Under Franz I, the **park** acquired its Romantic aspect with islands, bridges and grottoes. The **Franzensburg** was also built on an island in the lake, and is a sort of theme park of the Middle Ages, complete with a jousting arena and a knightly crypt. Laxenburg has recently been restored and makes an unusual excursion that might well appeal to children.

Heiligenkreuz★

(*The Cistercian monastery of Heiligenkreuz lies some 30km/19 miles south-west of Vienna in the Wienerwald and, together with Mayerling, see below, is reached by Bus 265 from Südtirolerplatz. Alternatively, group tours are available from travel agencies such as Vienna Sightseeing.*) The monastery **church★** was originally Romanesque, with a later stunning Gothic choir and unusual stained glass dating to 1300. Baroque ornamentation was added in the 18C by Giovanni Giuliani (the carved choir stalls, the plague column and fountain in the courtyard), who lived here as a working guest of the Order until his death. The name 'Heiligenkreuz' refers to a fragment of the True Cross brought back from the Crusades by Leopold V. In the well-house you can see portraits of other members of the Babenberg dynasty, and there is a Babenberg tomb in the chapter house. (*To see all the sights you must join a guided tour, of which there are five daily, from*

9-11.30am and 1.30-5pm Apr-Oct, or 1.30-4pm Nov-Mar.)

Mayerling

(6km/3.8 miles from Heiligenkreuz, reached by Bus 265 from Südtirolerplatz.)
The former imperial hunting lodge at Mayerling, its chief interest is that Crown Prince Rudolf committed suicide here (killing his lover, Marie Vetsera, at the same time) on 29 January 1889. Franz Joseph had the lodge demolished and a Carmelite nunnery erected on the site as a memorial. The neo-Gothic chapel may be visited and contains some devotional objects of Franz Joseph and Elisabeth. In a side room is preserved some of the furniture that Rudolf had in his hunting lodge, together with other souvenirs of his life.

The plague column stands in the centre of the courtyard at Heiligenkreuz.

WEATHER

The climate of Vienna is influenced by the overlap of the oceanic and continental regions at this point of Central Europe, which can lead to some dramatically rapid changes in the weather. Generally speaking, fronts arrive from the Atlantic seaboard in the north-west, but there are also icy spells in winter when the prevailing influence comes from the Russian steppe to the north-east. High summer is rather warm, with temperatures nudging 30°C (86°F) in July and August, while the winters are correspondingly cold (sub-zero for most of January with plenty of snow).

The summer months are the wettest, although November and December can also be quite wet, with drizzle more usual in spring and autumn. The Vienna basin (*Wiener Becken*) is kept free of the worst effects of pollution by the prevailing 'Wiener Wind', not to be confused with the dreaded *Föhn*, a warm wind sweeping off the Alps and causing migraines and circulation problems in those who are susceptible.

CALENDAR OF EVENTS

Vienna is famed for its rich music life, and the rolling programme of events throughout the year reflects this.
1 January
The **New Year's Day Concert** of the Wiener Philharmoniker takes place in the Musikverein. It is almost impossible to get tickets as the Viennese *beau monde* and the diplomatic community take precedence, but you can watch it live on television. If you want to go, write at least a year in advance to

the Musikverein, Bösendorfer Strasse 12,
A-1010, Wien. Another regular fixture for
New Year's Eve is the performance of
Johann Strauss's *Die Fledermaus* at the
Staatsoper (tickets from Bundestheater-
verband, Goethegasse 1, A-1010, Wien).

January-February
Fasching is carnival season in Vienna. The
most fashionable event is
the **Opernball**, which
attracts international
celebrities or publicity
seekers. The
demonstrations of the
1960s and 1970s that
used to be a feature of
the Opernball have gone
and the event (now
televised) has become a
typically 20C exercise in
harmless snobbery and
vicarious living.

March-April
The spring programme
of the **Viennale**, an
internationally
renowned film festival.

Mid-May to mid-June
The biggest arts festival
of the year, **Die Wiener
Festwochen**, consists
mostly of performances
by international soloists
and orchestral concert
series, as well as drama
and dance events.

15 May-end September
There is a *son et lumière* show in the gardens
of the Belvedere Palace, starting at 9.30pm
(9pm in September).

*The drummers set
the pace for the
carnival procession.*

June to mid-September
The popular **Wiener Musik-Sommer (Klangbogen Wien)** allows access to many palaces, castles and churches which are normally not open, for performances of concerts and recitals. For several weeks in mid summer, opera and orchestral classics are screened free in front of the Rathaus (City Hall) after sunset.

October
The autumn programme of the **Viennale** film festival.

November-December
Christmas markets are held in front of the Neues Rathaus, and in Freyung, Spittelberg and Heiligenkreuzerhof.

ACCOMMODATION

There is a wide choice of accommodation in Vienna, with some extra facilities such as student dormitories becoming available in the summer months. **Austrian National Tourist Offices** supply extensive lists of hotels and pensions, and the **Vienna Tourist Board** issues a comprehensive detailed listing – available from **Tourist Information Offices** at the end of the Autobahn A1 and A2, at railway stations, at Schwechat International Airport and at the bureau at Kärntner Strasse 38 and Stephansplatz.

The main choice to be made with hotels is whether you want to be inside the Ringstrasse in the Inner City (the ancient city centre), or outside it. Since city transport is good and taxis are reasonably priced, being outside the centre is not necessarily a disadvantage. There are, for example, some delightful places to stay in a leafy suburb like Hietzing, or in the districts to the north-west (Währing and Döbling).

Single rooms in hotels do not come cheaply and there seems to be a diminishing supply of them. During peak season prices are at their highest and booking is essential. Prices, per double room per night, with breakfast, are as follows:

5 star: over ATS 4 000

4 star: ATS 3 000-4 000

3 star: ATS 1 500-3 000

2 star: ATS 600-1 500

1 star: under ATS 600

Recommendations

Inexpensive ATS600–1 000

There are also eight **youth hostels** (information from the **Österreichischer Jugendherbergverband** ☎ 533 53 53, Fax: 535 08 61; or obtain the leaflet entitled *Youth Hostels and Camping Sites* from the tourist information offices).

Academia (☎ 401 76 10) and **Aquila** (☎ 405 52 35/0) at Pfeilgasse 3A and 1A respectively, and the **Atlas** (Lerchenfelder Strasse 1-3, ☎ 521 78/0) are three seasonal hotels providong cheap accommodation, but these may be more suitable for young people who do not require cosseting.

Zur Wiener Staatsoper (Krugerstrasse 11, ☎ 513 12 74) A small informal hotel in a sumptuous Viennese city house, with period furniture.

Landhaus Fuhrgassl-Huber (Rathstrasse 24, Neustift am Walde, ☎ 440 30 33) A very attractive pension located in the wine village of Neustift am Walde, which makes up for its distance from the centre with rustic charm.

Pension Pertschy (Habsburgergasse 5, ☎ 534 49) A family hotel in a 250-year-old Baroque palace, with Louis XV-style furniture.

ENJOYING YOUR VISIT

Pension Franz (Währingerstrasse 12,
☎ 34 36 37) is a private family hotel
furnished in turn-of-the-century style.

Moderate ATS1 200–1 800
Vienna has numerous **pensions**. In the Inner
City there are some pleasant ones, although
those in fashionable areas around the
Graben will not be very cheap.
Pension Nossek (Graben 17, ☎ 533 70 41).
Conveniently situated in the Graben.
Hotel-Pension Élite (Wipplingerstrasse 32,
☎ 533 25 18/0) Has some spacious rooms, is
moderately priced and conveniently located
in the western half of the Inner City.
Hotel Wandl (Petersplatz 9, ☎ 534 55)
A very traditional smaller hotel right in the
centre.
Theaterhotel (Josefstädter Strasse 22,
☎ 405 36 48) A modernised inner city hotel
close to the Ringstrasse.
Am Stefansplatz (Stephansplatz 9,
☎ 53 40 50) Situated right opposite the
Stephansdom, with rooms all facing the
front with a view of the cathedral.
König von Ungarn (Schulerstrasse 10,
☎ 51 58 40) A comfortable small hotel with
an 'Old Vienna' atmosphere; part of the
buildings include the Figarohaus and it is
well located, only a stone's throw from St
Stephen's.
Römischer Kaiser (Annagasse 16 ☎ 512 77
51) A small Baroque palace with true period
atmosphere.
Biedermeier im Sünnhof (Landstrasser,
Hauptstrasse 28, ☎ 71 87 10) More
expensive. Notable for its elegant conversion
of a huge Biedermeier block.
Hotel Jäger (Hernalser Hauptstrasse 187,
☎ 486 66 20) Good for families with children.

102

The entrance to the famous Hotel Sacher.

Hotel Residenz Cottage in Döbling (Hasenauerstrasse 12, ☎ 319 25 71) A turn-of-the-century villa in a residential district outside the city centre.

Moderate-Expensive ATS 1 800–2 500
Altstadt Vienna (Kirchengasse 41, ☎ 526 33 99/0) Offering nice local views across the rooftops.
Kärntnerhof (Grashofgasse 4, next to Heiligenkreuzerhof, ☎ 512 19 23) Reasonable facilities.
Kaiserin Elisabeth (Weihburggasse 3, ☎ 515 26) Good facilities and comfortable rooms.
Hotel am Schubertring (Schubertring 11, ☎ 71 70 20) Comfortable; a favourite with visiting musicians.

Expensive ATS2 500–4 000

The fairly numerous luxury hotels of Vienna all meet the highest world standards, many of them having been recently refurbished.

Hotel Sacher (Philharmoniker Strasse 4, ☎ 514 56) The well-heeled visitor may like to try this five star hotel with local Viennese flair.

Palais Schwarzenberg (Schwarzenbergplatz 9, ☎ 798 45 15) A former royal palace dating from the 18C, individually furnished with anitques.

Hotel Imperial (Kärntner Ring 16, ☎ 501 10) This will require deep pockets, but is the last word in 19C elegance.

ANA Grand Hotel (Kärntner Ring 9, ☎ 515 80) A state-of-the-art modern hotel.

Radisson SAS Palais Hotel (Parkring 14-16, ☎ 515 17) Created out of a 19C Ringstrassen palace.

Vienna Plaza (Schottenring 11, ☎ 313 90) An attractive hotel, run by Hilton Hotels.

FOOD AND DRINK

There is an enormous selection of restaurants in Vienna, ranging from the gourmet, through what is known as 'good bourgeois cooking' (*gute bürgerliche Küche*), to the cheaper cafés serving limited hot food, self-service restaurants, pastry shops (*Konditoreien*), sandwich bars and *Wurstelstände* (street kiosks selling sausages, beer and soft drinks). A Viennese speciality are the *Heurigen* selling cheap local wine and simple food (*see* p92).

First courses are strong in the soup department (*Eierschwammerlsuppe* – chanterelle soup, *Frittatensuppe* – clear broth with crêpes), but also offer some interesting local starters that are worth a try, notably *Sulz*, which is brawn in aspic.

The **main courses** include well-known Viennese favourites such as *Wiener Schnitzel* (the true one made with veal, but more usually pork) and *Tafelspitz* (tender boiled beef). Another common beef dish is *Zwiebelrostbraten* (a rump steak with crispy onions). Pork comes in many forms, including smoked (*geselchtes*), as loin (*Jungfernbraten*), as shoulder (*Karree*), or boiled with horseradish (*Krenfleisch*). Some dishes are rather heavy and perhaps more suitable as winter fare, such as *Blunzen* (black pudding), *Bauernschmaus* (mixed meats with dumplings and sauerkraut), and *Hirschragout* (venison stew). Bohemian influence is evident in the excellent dumplings; try *Selchfleischknödel* (smoked pork dumplings), or *Grammelknödel* (dumplings filled with pork scratchings), as

The Griensteidl Café, one of Vienna's traditional stopping off places for a coffee and pastry.

well as plum and apricot versions.

Fresh fish are inevitably freshwater species, such as *Fogosch* (pike-perch) or *Karpfen* (carp), but Vienna now has a number of restaurants specialising in sea-fish and shellfish brought from further afield. Common vegetables are *Speckbohnen* (beans with flecks of bacon), *Fisolen* (runner beans), *Blaukraut* (red cabbage), and various types of potato dish (*Purée, Frites* and *Petersilienkartoffeln* – boiled potatoes turned in fat with parsley garnish).
For **dessert** (*Mehlspeisen*), pancakes (*Palatschinken*) are often on the menu and may be filled with chocolate or apricot jam. *Zwetschkenknödel* (plum dumplings) are highly recommended, as are the steamed puddings known as *Aufläufe,* which is also the word for soufflé.

Drinks
Beer (*Bier*) is widely available, the two local breweries of Ottakringer and Schwechat supplying a range of bottled or cask beers which, however, do not begin to match the quality of Prague or Bavarian beers.
The **wine** served in *Heurigen* is an acquired taste, being young and white, often slightly petillant. The classic Austrian white wine is the *Grüner Veltliner*, which can be excellent and certainly matches the best Italian whites. Of the reds, it is worth trying the local *Blauer Portugieser* and the *Blaufränkisch,* full-bodied and satisfying wines at their best.

Some Recommended Restaurants
Luxury
Steirereck (Rasumofskygasse 2, ☎ 713 31 68) is considered by many to be the best restaurant in Vienna and serves a

version of nouvelle cuisine. For traditional Austrian cuisine it is hard to choose between the **Restaurant im Palais Schwarzenberg** (Schwarzenbergplatz 9, ☎ 798 45 15/600), the **Drei Husaren** (Weihburggasee 4, ☎ 512 10 92) and **Korso bei der Oper** (Mahlerstrasse 2, ☎ 515 160), the last-named being very distinguished. Seafood is available at **Kervansaray** (Mahlerstrasse 9, ☎ 512 88 43), with its **Hummerbar** (lobster bar) on the first floor.

Medium-priced

One of the most popular restaurants, right in the centre of the city and with a beautiful inner courtyard, is **Haas & Haas** (Stephensplatz 4, ☎ 513 19 16). For a typical old Viennese restaurant try **Zur ebenen Erde und erster Stock** (Burggasse 13, ☎ 523 62 54). **Hauswirth** (Otto-Bauer-Gasse 20, ☎ 587 12 61) has traditional atmosphere and food, with a pleasant garden for diners. Good food is on offer at **Zu den drei Hacken** (Singerstrasse 28, ☎ 512 58 95), **Zur Tabakspfeife** (Goldschmiedgasse 4, ☎ 533 72 86) and **Bei Max** (Landhausgasse 2, ☎ 533 73 59). The **Hietzinger Bräu** (Auhofstrasse 1, ☎ 877 70 87) serves traditional Viennese beef cuisine. Very traditional and good value is **Figlmüller** (Wollzeile 5 – in the alley – ☎ 512 61 77). New Viennese cuisine is found in **Vikerl's Lokal** (Würffelgasse 4, ☎ 894 34 30), a small, cosy wood-panelled restaurant, and the excellent intimate restaurant, **Fadinger** (Wipplingerstrasse 29, ☎ 533 43 41).

Wine cellars

Cellars which serve a limited range of food and provide romantic ambience include the

Augustinerkeller (Augustinerstrasse 1), the
Melker Stiftskeller (Schottengasse 3) and
the **Esterhazykeller** (Haarhof 1).

Cafés

Cafés are a much-loved feature of Viennese
life, and many a happy hour can be spent
with just a coffee and an *Apfelstrudel*, watching
the world go by. Congenial are the **Tirolerhof**
(Tegetthoffstrasse 8), **Diglas** (Wollzeile 10),
Schwarzenberg (Kärntner Ring 17), **Café
Landtmann** (Dr.-Karl-Lueger-Ring 4) and
Café Griensteidl (Michaelerplatz 2), but
there are many others. Those a little off the
beaten track offer better value for meals
(**Café Ministerium** at Georg-Coch-Platz 4,
Café Sperl at Gumpendorfer Strasse 11).

Konditoreien

Konditoreien (pastry shops and confectioners)
also have a long tradition in the city. The
most famous is **Demel** (Kohlmarkt 14), but
some are less overrun with tourists and may
be more sympathetic (**Heiner** at Wollzeile 9,
Kurcafé Konditorei Oberlaa at Neuer Markt
16). **Sluka**, underneath the arcades of the
City Hall (Rathausplatz 8), is pleasantly
insulated from the hurly-burly of the city.
The **Aida** chain (many branches inside and
outside the Inner City) is somewhat cheaper
than the noble *Konditoreien*, but has
excellent fare. Especially pleasant in winter
is **Lehmann**, on the fashionable Graben
(Graben 12).

Self-service and fast food

Self-service and fast food takes many forms
in the city. The **Naschmarkt** chain of self-
service restaurants offers Austrian food at
reasonable prices and a pleasant setting

(Schwarzenbergplatz 16 and Schottengasse 1). There are similarly well-designed self-service places in the **Ringstrassen-Galerien** (Kärntner Ring) and the **Rosenberger** (in Führichgasse), but they are not all that cheap. The **Nordsee** chain of fish restaurants (Kohlmarkt, Kärntner Strasse and elsewhere) can be recommended for a reasonably priced, healthy meal. Lastly, the sandwich bar **Trzesniewski** (Dorotheer-gasse 1) is a Viennese institution worth visiting for its large selection of open sandwiches, while another good sandwich bar in the centre is **Superimbiss Duran** (Rotenturmstrasse 11).

Stop off at a good café-konditorei for cakes and confectionary to sample and take home.

SHOPPING

The two great shopping streets in Vienna are the **Kärntner Strasse** (roughly equivalent to London's Bond Street) and the **Mariahilfer Strasse** (more like London's Oxford Street).

The Kärntner Strasse is a pedestrian zone, with numerous fine shops offering fashion, antiquities, textiles and fabrics, glassware, books and CDs. **Lobmeyr** (No 26) is a famous glassmaker and has a selection of attractive historical designs. **Backhausen** (No 33) sells material with Wiener Werkstätte designs. Gifts, ornaments and costume jewellery to traditional designs may be found at **Österreichische Werkstätten** (No 6), while books about Vienna (some in English) are at **Georg Prachner** (No 30) and CDs next door at **EMI Austria**. However, the biggest selection of books in English (including a substantial section on Vienna and Austria) is to be found at the **British Bookshop** (Weihburgggase 24-26).

In the Mariahilfer Strasse are the big stores such as **Herzmansky**, **Gerngross** and **Leiner**, which have made vigorous efforts to revolutionise their formerly somewhat old-fashioned image in recent years. There is also a **Virgin Megastore** at Nos 37-39, and numerous smaller shops (usually in the unpretentious side-streets round about) which sell electrical goods, computers, cameras and the like, often at more favourable prices than elsewhere.

ENTERTAINMENT AND NIGHTLIFE

An indispensable aid to enjoying your visit is the monthly **Wien Programm** (free from tourist offices and ticket agencies). It lists all the month's events (opera, concerts, jazz, theatre, exhibitions, guided tours on foot), together with details of venues and where to obtain tickets. Ticket agents charge a hefty commission of up to 25%, so it is worth

Vienna is a city of music – from opera to bands in street cafés.

making the effort to go straight to the venue or ticket office whenever possible. The pre-booking office for the state theatres (Staatsoper, Volksoper, Burgtheater, Akademietheater) is at Hanuschgasse 3 (no commission is charged). Booking with credit cards by phone is possible, but only from seven days before the performance (☎ 513 15 13).

Informal nightlife (bars, beer halls, fringe theatre, jazz, dancing, cabaret) is concentrated mainly in the so-called **Bermuda Triangle**, an area of narrow old streets between the Ruprechtskirche and Rotenturmstrasse (Rabensteig, Seitenstettengasse, Judengasse). Favoured locales are **Krah Krah** (Rabensteig 8), the **Roter Engel** (Rabensteig 5) and the fashionable restaurant with an interior by a well-known modern designer, **Salzamt** (Ruprechtsplatz 1, booking essential, ☎ 533 53 32). **Pfudl** (Bäckerstr. 22) is a bar

which has become a Viennese institution.
Altes Fassl (Ziegelofengasse 37) is a typical
suburban Beisl, housed in a Biedermeier
period house, while another suburban bar,
Pötsch (Favoritenstr. 61), has a huge range
of dishes and similarly sized portions.

Discos come and go, as elsewhere, but one
that seems to have stood the test of time is
U4 (Schönbrunner Strasse 222).

SPORTS

Vienna is well provided with *swimming baths*,
some of which are worth visiting for their
architectural features (e.g. the art deco

Amalienbad on Reumannplatz, last stop on
the U1), the **Kurzentrum Oberlaa** (last stop
on Tram 67 and a place to spend the whole
day), or the state-of-the-art sports pool in the
Stadthalle (Tram 49 to Urban-Loritz-Platz).
Danube bathing is possible on the dead arm
of the river (Alte Donau) at **Gänsehäufel**
(Moissigasse 21) and also at the
Arbeiterstrandbad in Floridsdorf
(Arbeiterstrandbadstrasse 91). The nude
bathing (in German: FKK) beach is also in
the Gänsehäufel area.

Skating is on offer in winter at the **Wiener
Eislaufverein** (Lothringerstrasse 22) and
there are numerous *tennis courts* (see under
Tennisplätze in the Yellow Pages or ask your
hotel concierge). *Golf* is slowly catching on
in Austria, although Viennese facilities at
Freudenau 65A and out in the 10th District
on the **Wienerberg** are only for those who
suffer withdrawal symptoms if deprived of
golf for more than a few days. *Bicycling* is
popular and there are bicycle routes
signposted along the Ringstrasse and
elsewhere. More adventurous excursion
routes may be obtained from the Tourist
Information Office at the City Hall
(Rathaus). Bicycle hire is possible (for
instance on the Donaupromenade at
Nussdorf, at the Floridsdorfer Brücke and in
the Prater).

The **Wienerwald★** (Vienna Woods) have
offered a tranquil and scenic retreat for the
Viennese and town-dwellers since the early
19C. Once the haunt of wolves and bears,
the woods today are less wild, but are
popular for walking and picnics. They can
be reached by public transport from the city,
and there are numerous marked *rambling*
routes through the woods.

*For a romantic
evening, what better
than a dinner-
cruise.*

THE BASICS

Before You Go

A valid passport or a personal identity card (for residents of the EU) is sufficient for entry into Austria. Citizens from Australia, Canada, New Zealand and the US may travel within Austria for up to three months without a visa providing they hold a valid passport. No vaccinations are necessary.

Getting There

By Air: There are regular international flights in and out of Vienna's Schwechat Airport ☎ 70 07 22 31/32 (24hrs).

Austrian Airlines, Austria's international airline, can be contacted at 10 Wardolf Street, 5th Floor, London W1V 4BQ ☎ (0171) 434 7300. The reservations number in Vienna is ☎ 17 89 Monday to Friday 8am-6pm; weekends and holidays 8am-5pm.

By Car: Vienna can be reached from Bavaria via the West Autobahn (A 1), from the south via the South Autobahn (A 2) and from the Hungarian border via the East Autobahn (A 4).

For information on the state of the roads ☎ 711 99 7 (24hrs). *See also* **Driving** and **Car Hire**

By Coach: Coach connections are available between Vienna and most Austrian cities and several major cities in Europe ☎ 523 30 00 or 711 01. The main bus station is at Wien Mitte. Eurolines runs regular bus services to Vienna from the UK and other European countries.

Information and bookings in the UK from 52 Grosvenor Gardens, London SW1W 0AU ☎ (0171) 730 8235.

By Train: International train connections link Vienna directly with several major European cities. Vienna has three international railway stations: Westbahnhof (Western Austria and Western Europe); Südbahnhof (Southern and Eastern Austria and Southern Europe); and Franz-Josefs-Bahnhof (Northern Austria and the Czech Republic).

For train information ☎ 17 17 (24hrs). For information about rail travel to Austria from the UK, ☎ 0990 848 848.

Arriving

The airport is 19km (11.8 miles) from the city centre. Express buses leave and depart from the City Air Terminal (Wien Mitte, Landstrasse) every 20 minutes during the day and from the Südbahnhof and Westbahnhof railway stations every 30 minutes. A train service also operates to Wien Mitte.

Note that taxis levy an airport surcharge.

Heldenplatz dramatically lit at night.

A-Z

Accidents and Breakdowns

For 24-hour breakdown service, call one of Austria's two automobile clubs: ARBÖ ☎ **123** or ÖAMTC ☎ **120**.

When travelling in a hire car, contact the rental firm in the event of an accident or breakdown.
See also **Driving**

Accommodation *see* p.100

Airports *see* **Getting There** p.114

Banks

Banks are usually open in Vienna 8am-12.30pm and 2.30-4.30pm Mondays, Tuesdays, Wednesdays and Fridays, and 8am-12.30pm and 1.30-5.30pm on Thursdays. They are closed on Saturdays and Sundays. Exchange offices at the airport and rail terminals are open daily 8am-10pm.

Bicycles

Cycling is an excellent way of getting around Vienna and special cycle lanes are designated on roads all over the city. Bicycles can be hired at all the main railway stations. Details of hire companies, plus other cycling information, is listed in the free leaflet for cyclists available at tourist information offices.

Breakdowns *see* **Accidents**

Buses *see* **Transport**

Camping

For details of campsites in and around Vienna contact the Austrian Camping Club, Schubertring 1-3, 1010 Vienna ☎ **431 711 99 ext 1272**.

Car Hire

International and local car hire companies are based in the city, mostly around the Ring, as well as at the airport. Make sure that collision damage waiver is included in the insurance. Automatics should be reserved in advance and are more expensive.

The lower age limit is 21, but few international companies hire to drivers under 23, or even 25. Drivers must have held their full licence for at least a year.

With the exception of Avis, there is an upper age limit of 60-65. Unless paying by credit card a substantial cash deposit is usually required. If you are driving a car that has obviously been hired, take extra precautions when parking it to deter thieves, and never leave anything of value inside. *See also* **Accidents and Breakdowns** and **Tourist Information Offices**

Children

Information of all kinds geared towards young people (mostly teenagers) is obtainable from Jugend-Info Wien 1, Dr-Karl-Renner-Ring/Bellaria-Passage, open Monday to Friday noon-7pm, Saturday 10am-7pm ☎ **526 46 37**.

Attractions in or near Vienna likely to appeal to children include:

Circus and Clown Museum, 2 Karmelitergasse 9 ☎ **211 06 02 127**.

The **Prater**, Praterstern. Parkland with a huge fairground, including the giant Ferris Wheel (*see* p.85).

Safari Park, Gänserndorf (30km/18.6 miles north-east of the city) ☎ **02282 702610**. Lots of animals and an Adventure Park with baby animals.

Schönbrunn Tiergarten, Schönbrunn Park. Vienna's zoo, formerly the Imperial Menagerie (*see* p.82).

Climate *see* **p.98**

Clothing

Warm clothes and non-slip shoes are essential in winter, when temperatures can be extremely low and the streets icy. Conversely, in mid-summer it can be very hot indeed, although evenings tend to be cool. Smart clothing will be required by concert or opera-goers.

Women's clothes

UK	8	10	12	14	16	18
Europe	34	36	38	40	42	44
US	6	8	10	12	14	16

Men's suits

UK/US	36	38	40	42	44	46
Europe	46	48	50	52	54	56

Men's shirts

UK/US	14	14.5	15	15.5	16	16.5	17
Europe	36	37	38	39/40	41	42	43

Men's shoes

UK	7	7.5	8.5	9.5	10.5	11
Europe	41	42	43	44	45	46
US	8	8.5	9.5	10.5	11.5	12

Women's shoes

UK	4.5	5	5.5	6	6.5	7
Europe	38	38	39	39	40	41
US	6	6.5	7	7.5	8	8.5

Consulates

Australia
Mattiellistrasse 2-4
☎ 512 85 80-0
Canada
Laurenzerberg 2
☎ 531 38 33 21
Ireland
Hilton Centre, Landstrasser
Hauptstrasse 2A ☎ 715 42 46
New Zealand
(Trade Development Board)
Springsiedelgasse 28
☎ 28 318 85 05
UK
Jaurésgasse 12 ☎ 714 6117
USA
Gartentaupromenade 2
☎ 313 39-0

Crime

There is no need to be unduly
concerned about serious crime
in Vienna, but it is advisable to
take sensible precautions and
be on your guard at all times.
• Carry as little money, and as
few credit cards, as possible,
and leave any valuables in the
hotel safe.
• Carry wallets and purses in
secure pockets inside your
outer clothing, wear body
belts, or carry handbags across
your body or under your arm.
• Cars can be a target for
opportunists, so never leave
your car unlocked.
• If you do have anything
stolen, report it immediately to
the local police and collect a
copy of the report so that you
can make an insurance claim.
• If your passport is stolen,
report it to your Consulate or
Embassy at once
(*see* **Consulates**).

Currency *see* **Money**

Customs and Entry Regulations

There is no limit on the impor-
tation into Austria of tax-paid
goods bought in an EU
country, provided they are for
personal consumption, with
the exception of alcohol and
tobacco which have fixed limits
governing them.

Disabled Visitors

The Vienna Tourist Board
produces a free booklet
(available from Austrian
Tourist Boards abroad)
entitled *Vienna for Guests with
Handicaps* which covers
transport, hotels, eating out,
sights, theatres and cinemas,
plus other information.

The *Michelin Red Guide
Europe* indicates which hotels
have facilities for the disabled.

In Britain, RADAR, at 12 City
Forum, 250 City Road, London
EC1V 8AF; ☎ (0171) 250 3222,
publishes fact sheets, as well as
an annual guide to facilities
and accommodation overseas.

Driving

Driving is not the best way of exploring Vienna as there are many one-way streets and tramways and parking is difficult. The Inner City (the heart of which is pedestrianised) has short-term parking only and tickets, obtainable at tobacconists, some banks, railway stations and Vienna Transport Authority offices, must be purchased in advance and displayed on the windscreen. Parking cards (enquire at your hotel) enable you to park for a whole day in the short-term zone.

Drivers should carry a full national or preferably international driving licence, insurance documents

Fiaker horses in Heldenplatz.

including a green card (no longer compulsory for EU members but strongly recommended), registration papers for the car, and a nationality sticker for the car rear.

The minimum age for driving is 18, and cars drive on the right.

The wearing of seat belts is compulsory.

Children under 12 are not allowed to travel in the front seats.

The blood alcohol limit is 0.8 per cent.

To travel on the Austrian Autobahns you have to buy a 3-month or yearly *Pickerl* (sticker). This can be purchased at the border and may be checked by the police at any time.

Speed limits are as follows:
• Maximum on built-up areas: 50kph/31mph
• Maximum outside built-up areas: 100kph/62mph
• Maximum on motorways: 130kph/81mph
• Cars pulling trailers (including caravans) are limited to a maximum of 80kph/50mph on roads and motorways.

Electric Current

The voltage in Austria is 220V. Sockets are of the two-pin variety and American appli-

ances will require a trans-
former.

Embassies *see* Consulates

Emergencies
Police: ☎ 133
Fire: ☎ 122
Ambulance: ☎ 144
Emergency doctor: ☎ 141

Etiquette
There are few differences in
culture that visitors need be
aware of but it is polite to
remember the following con-
ventions:
• Use the 'Sie' form of address
if you speak German.
• When invited into a private
home, always take a gift for the
hostess and some token for any
young children in the
household.
• If you know the title of the
person you are addressing, use
it.

Guidebooks *see* Maps

Health
UK nationals should carry a
Form E111 which is produced
by the Department of Health,
and which entitles the holder
to free urgent treatment for
accident or illness in EU
countries (forms are available
from post offices in Britain).
Before consulting a doctor, this

international certificate must
be exchanged for a valid
Certificate of Health Insurance
(Krankenschein) at Wiener
Gebietskrankenkasse,
10 Wienerbergstrasse 15-19,
Monday to Thursday 8am-2pm;
Friday 8am-1pm. If this is not
possible, give the doctor your
international certificate and
obtain the Certificate of
Health Insurance afterwards,
which must then be sent to the
doctor.

All foreign nationals,
including those from the UK,
are advised to take out comprehensive insurance cover, and to
keep any bills, receipts and
invoices to support any claim.

Hospitals are obliged to treat
acute cases, such as injury.

The addresses of specialists
and practitioners of all kinds
can be found in the Vienna
telephone book under the
heading 'Ärzte'.

Hours *see* Opening Hours

Information *see* Tourist
Information Offices

Language
German is the first language of
the vast majority of Austrians,
and, although English is widely
understood and spoken by
people employed in tourist-
related industries in Vienna,

Yes / Ja	Water / Das Wasser
No / Nein	White wine / Der Weisswein
Please / Bitte	Red wine / Der Rotwein
Thank you / Danke	Beer / Das Bier
Good morning / Guten Morgen	How much? / Wieviel?
Good evening / Guten Abend	Bill / Die Rechnung
Goodbye / Auf Wiedersehen	Do you speak English? / Sprechen Sie Englisch?
Large / Gross	Where is … ? / Wo ist … ?
Small / Klein	I don't understand / Ich verstehe nicht
Menu / Die Speisekarte	

an attempt at the native language is always appreciated.

Lost Property

Lost property bureau, 9 Wasagasse 22 ☎ 31 44 92; open Monday to Friday 8am-noon.

For items lost on public transport, call ☎ 79 0943 500 within three days of losing the item.

Maps

The Michelin Road Map **No 926** Austria, which covers the whole country, will help with route-planning and when making excursions, and also has a street plan of Vienna. The *Michelin Green Guide Vienna* includes full information on all the key sights and attractions in the city, with detailed maps and background information. The *Michelin Red Guide Europe* provides details of accommodation and has a list of selected restaurants.

Medical Care see Health

Money

The Austrian unit of currency is the Austrian Schilling (abbreviated as ATS internationally, ÖS, or S, in Austria) which is divided into 100 Groschen. Bank notes come in denominations of 20, 50, 100, 500, 1 000 and 5 000 Schillings; coins come in 2, 5, 10, 50 Groschen and in 1, 5, 10 and 20 Schillings.

There is no limit to the amount of Schillings or other foreign currency that may be taken in or out of Austria.

ECU cards and international credit cards provide immediate access to cash from cash machines 24 hours a day. Payment can be made nearly everywhere by EU card, Eurocheque or any of the major credit card companies.

Money can be changed at a bank or a bureau de change; exchange rates vary. Automated changing machines can be found all over the city.

Newspapers

Most large hotels and news-stands stock the major European dailies and the *International Herald Tribune,* published in Paris, which offers the latest stock market news from America as well as world news.

The fortnightly *Vienna Reporter,* published in English, lists what's on where in the city and *Falter,* one of the weeklies, has an events section; both are widely available at bookshops and news-stands.

Opening Hours

Shops normally open 8/9am-6pm Monday to Friday, and 9-noon on Saturdays. Many shops are open until 5pm on the first Saturday in the month. Shops in the Westbahn-hof and Südbahnhof are open 7am-11pm.

Chemists (*Apotheke*) open 8-noon and 2-6pm; they close on Saturday afternoons and Sundays. Lists of chemists which are open late or on Sundays are displayed in every branch.

Museums and galleries There are no standard opening times but most are open from Tuesday to Sunday, 9/10am-5/6pm. The Vienna Tourist Board can supply a leaflet giving full details of all Vienna's museums and galleries.
See also **Banks** and **Post Offices**

Photography

Good-quality film and camera equipment are available in Vienna, and facilities for fast processing are plentiful, although this is often expensive.

Before taking photographs in museums and art galleries it is wise to check with staff as photography is often restricted in these places.

Police

Police stations can be found all over the city, identifiable by a red/white/red sign.

Post Offices

Vienna's main post office, Vienna 1, Fleischmarkt 19, and

the post offices at Westbahnhof, Südbahnhof and Franz-Josefs-Bahnhof are open 24 hours daily.

Branch post offices are open from Monday to Friday, 8am-noon and 2pm-6pm; some remain open through lunchtime and also open on Saturday 7am-7pm.

Stamps are sold at post offices and at newsagents. *See also* **Telephones**

Public Holidays

New Year's Day: 1 January
Epiphany: 6 January
Easter Monday
Labour Day: 1 May
Ascension Day
Whit Monday
Corpus Christi: 2nd Thursday
    after Whitsun
Assumption Day: 15 August
National Day: 26 October
All Saints' Day: 1 November
Immaculate Conception:
    8 December
Christmas Day: 25 December
Boxing Day: 26 December

Public Transport *see* Transport

Religion

Roman Catholic services for visitors to Vienna are held in several languages in the Votive Church on Saturdays at 6pm, on Sundays and public holidays at 9.30am (in German) and at 11am (in English).

Information about services in other churches and denominations can be obtained from the *Grüss Gott,* available from tourist information offices.

Smoking

In general, this is still widely tolerated in the city, although the trend is gradually changing. Smoking is prohibited on public transport and in certain public buildings but is common in bars and restau-

Café in the Graben.

rants; there may be some non-
smoking areas.

Stamps *see* Post Offices

Taxis *see* Transport

Telephones
There are numerous
telephone kiosks in Vienna:
most take telephone cards
which can be purchased at
tobacconists and post offices.
Some kiosks in the Kohlmarkt
area take credit cards. Calls can
also be made inside post
offices, where payment is made
at the end of the call.

As in most countries,
telephone calls made from
hotels may be more straightfor-
ward and convenient, but they
are more expensive.

The international dialing
code for Vienna is ☎ 0043 1
Operator: ☎ 1616
Directory enquiries: ☎ 1611
International enquiries:
☎ 1612 (Germany);
☎ 1613 (Europe);
☎ 1614 (rest of the world)
Telegrams: ☎ 190
Country codes are as follows:
Australia: ☎ 00 61
Canada: ☎ 00 1
Ireland: ☎ 00 353
New Zealand: ☎ 00 64
UK: ☎ 00 44
USA: ☎ 00 1

Time Difference
Vienna is on Central European
time, one hour ahead of GMT.

Tipping
A service charge of 10-15 per
cent is included in all hotel
and restaurant bills, but a
further gratuity is usually
expected.

Tourist Information Offices
Vienna Tourist Board A-1025
Vienna ☎ 211 140.

Official tourist information
office and room reservations,
Vienna 1, Kärntner Strasse 38,
open daily 9am-7pm.

Austrian National Tourist
Office in Vienna,
Margaretenstrasse 1, A-1040
Vienna ☎ (1) 588 66 0.

Austrian National Tourist
Offices abroad:
Australia
36 Carrington Street, 1st Floor,
Sydney, NSW 2000
☎ (02) 9299 3621
Canada
2 Bloor Street East, Suite 3330,
Toronto, Ontario M4W 1A8
☎ (416) 967 3381
Ireland
Merrion Hall, Strand Road,
Sandymount, PO Box 2506,
Dublin ☎ (01) 283 04 88
UK
30 St George Street, London
W1R 0AL
☎ (0171) 629 0461

USA
PO Box 1142, New York, NY
10108-1142 ☎ (212) 944 6880

Tours
However you would like to see
the sights, Vienna has a tour to
offer.

Vienna Guide Service,
A-1190 Vienna, Sommer-
haidenweg 124 ☎ 440 30 94-0:
offers guides for half or whole
days. Walking tours with a
variety of themes covering
culture, history, architecture,
etc are available; contact
tourist information offices for
a programme.

Vienna Sightseeing Tours
☎ 712 46 83-0: sightseeing by
streetcar; May to October only
☎ 587 31 86.

Vienna Bike ☎ 319 12 58:
sightseeing by bicycle.

Boat trips are available from
the DDSG (Danube Steamship
Company) from April to
October, ☎ 727 50-451.

Transport
U-Bahn, Trams and Buses
Vienna is covered by an integrated transport network
consisting of underground
trains (U-Bahn), trams
(Strassenbahn) and buses. The
central office of the Vienna
Transport Authority (Wiener
Linien) is in the underpass
(Opern Passage) at Karlsplatz,
where maps and other information about the transport
system are available. Maps
showing the routes of the five
colour-coded U-Bahn lines
criss crossing the city are also
posted on platforms.

Several types of ticket can be
purchased but the most eco-
nomical option is to obtain a
ticket that covers the length of
your stay. Tickets are sold at
newsagents and offices of the
Vienna Transport Authority at
main underground and tram
stations. Individual tickets are
expensive, the ticket machine
on the trams are not easy to
master and a lot of small
change is needed. Tickets
bought in advance must be
punched in a blue ticket-can-
celling machine before
boarding the bus or train.

The *Wien-Karte* (Vienna

Delicious Viennese confectionary.

Card) is well worth buying. It can be used on the underground, bus or tram network for up to 72 hours; it also entitles the bearer to reductions on certain sights and guided tours, and to discounts in some restaurants and cafés. The card can be bought at hotels, tourist information offices or at Vienna Transport's sales counters and information offices.

Generally, underground trains, trams and buses operate from 5.30am-12 midnight. Between 12.30am and 4.30am, 22 bus lines operate. Nightline stations can be recognised by a circular green sign bearing a white N.

Children under 6 travel free, as do children (including visitors) under 15 on Sundays, public holidays and during the

Vienna school holidays (one week in February, at Easter and 28 June to 31 August); an ID photo is required as proof of age.

Taxis can be found at the airport, all stations and at taxi ranks around the city. They can also be summoned by telephoning ☎ **31 300**, ☎ **40 100**, ☎ **60 160** or ☎ **81 400**, but will rarely stop when hailed in the street. There are additional charges for radio service, at night, Sundays and public holidays and journeys to or from the airport.

TV and Radio

Cable and satellite television is widely available in the larger, more expensive hotels. There are no English-language programmes on Austrian television.

Radio programmes are broadcast in English from 6am-7pm on Blue Danube Radio, on 92.9 MHZ.

Vaccinations see **Before You Go p.114**

Youth Hostels see **Accommodation p.100**

Vintage tram.

INDEX

INDEX